Arden's Housing Library

9.

The Series Editors of Arden's Housing Library are **Andrew Arden QC** and **Caroline Hunter**. The team of expert authors is drawn from the members of Arden Chambers and other practitioners.

Arden's Housing Library provides accessible guidance to the details of housing rights and duties for those involved in the management of social housing. It breaks up the whole subject into digestible segments and approaches each topic from the perspective of its practical application. Information about other titles in the Library is given at the back of this book.

Desmond Kilcoyne is a practising barrister at Arden Chambers in London, specialising in housing, landlord and tenant, and local government law.

Leaseholder Management

Law and Practice
in the Management
of Social Housing

Desmond Kilcoyne, Barrister

Published in Great Britain 1997 by
Lemos & Crane
20 Pond Square
Highgate
London N6 6BA
Telephone: 0181 348 8263
Fax: 0181 347 5740
Email: admin@lemos.demon.co.uk

ISBN 1-898001-10-3

A CIP catalogue record for this book is available from
the British Library

Design by Mick Keates
Typeset by Concise Artisans, London
Printed and bound by Redwood Books, Trowbridge

Contents

PART II

Foreword

by Andrew Arden QC

It is an odd title: *Leaseholder Management* – as if leaseholders were a special breed, with special problems and special needs. If that is the impression that the title gives, then it is quite right: in a series addressed to social landlords, uppermost in our minds are tenants conventionally so-called, weekly or monthly, whose recourse to the subsidised sector reflects the shortage of affordable housing to rent or buy privately, out of the grasp of too much of the population. We come to social housing, then, with – consciously or unconsciously – something of a preconception: that the occupiers need to be provided for; that while they may be capable of making choices about their housing – organisation, design, maintenance – it is a choice that has to be *given* (with the prospect of being able to take the choice away again should its exercise not meet with approval or should the greater good require); that even if they have security, it is one conditional on fixed behavioural criteria, subject to the jurisdiction of the courts.

This will sound harsh. It *is* harsh, because few if any in social housing would subscribe to these attitudes, and certainly not *en bloc*. It is not something that is being attributed to any one individual. Yet it is there, lurking, and it informs our responses: hence, under the Housing Act 1996, Part V, Chapter III, it is only introductory, secure and assured tenants – and those being housed as homeless under Part VII – who are vulnerable to arrest for anti-social behaviour, as if – magically – tenants who purchase a lease, e.g. under the right to buy or right to acquire – or their friends, relatives, visitors or children – cease to be capable of bad behaviour, and the payment has secured not merely property but character, freedoms the occupier can (now he has paid for it) be trusted not to abuse.

This is mirrored in law. Owner-occupation (including long leasehold occupation) *does* carry greater freedom. Rarely is it expressed so bluntly, and there are occasional judicial *dicta* which recognise that statutory security for life is not much less of an asset than outright proprietorship: in practice, however, owner-occupiers are led to expect – and therefore come to expect – much greater freedom from external supervision than tenants, both as a matter of law and (which is perhaps more significant) as a matter of *application* of law. Thus, to take the easiest example, the courts will strive and strain to avoid forfeiting a lease worth some tens of thousands of pounds, on account of e.g. arrears of service charges which may themselves reach five figures, where they would not hesitate to make an outright order against a tenant. Likewise, the court expects much greater accountability of managers to owner-occupiers than it does to tenants.

It is, of course, in no way wrong to expect such assets to be protected and interests to be respected; likewise, it is not wrong to expect owner-occupiers to want to exercise the freedom they believe they have acquired to do what they will with their own properties, loudly proclaim their rights quietly to enjoy their homes, fiercely to demand in exchange for a payment for services that is clearly marked out from their mortgages and ground rent a pound for pound, *perceptible* return, and of course – perhaps the greatest freedom of all – to move home at will.

What may be more doubtful is the extent to which we adequately allow these rights to tenants, in practice and not just in law or in theory. What may be equally in (serious) doubt is whether the bulk of public housing from which a portion has now transferred to owner-occupation – particularly that part of it which is leasehold (flats, maisonettes, some houses on estates) – is capable of providing occupiers with the freedoms they (perfectly properly) believed they were acquiring.

It is evident that there is a considerable mismatch between expectation and reality: service charges are not uncommonly out of control (and out of reach); maintenance of common parts and estates which must in part be funded from ring-fenced, decreasingly subsidised Housing Revenue Accounts, is often well below that which even the most creative estate agent can advertise in terms of "desirable amenities and environment"; neighbour relations may have been subject to added strain as a result of the differences in tenure; there are management problems few could handle with ease, and that *no one* (managers in the social housing sector or otherwise) has been trained to deal with.

This can sometimes lead to treatment of owner-occupiers which is positively adverse (or even adversarial) in a context in which there are inadequate resources, and owner-occupied public housing remains something of a novelty (the right to buy is less than 20 years – less than a generation – old); managers – unable to please all of the people all of the time – can sometimes adopt a resentment which they believe the (equally dissatisfied) tenants feel (and which doubtless some of them do). The mix is a breeding-ground for discontent: the notion that occupiers can happily exist cheek-by-jowl under differing tenures, with different interests and different rights, is patently absurd – the carpet is always brighter on the other side of the party-wall; the task of managing it is unenviable.

That is what this book is about. It is, as the other books in Arden's Housing Library, about providing the manager of a social landlord's property with part of the wherewithal to do his or her job, by providing him or her with the correct legal starting-point. It may well be said that management is not "about law", or need not suffer recourse to litigation. That is right. Unless management, however, is aware of, and absorbs, the legal rights and duties by which its activities are governed, policy and practice choices are vulnerable to disruption at the suit of an individual who asserts an absolute entitlement that may be inconsistent or even incompatible with what the landlord wants to do (including those voluntary programmes intended to even out the discrepancies between the tenures, and the shortfall in resources, e.g. programmes of maintenance or improvement, choices about decoration and design of blocks of flats or estates, rules and regulations by which occupation is to be governed, etc.).

This point was made in the Forewords to the twin publications on housing conditions in this series – A. Kilpatrick, *Repairs and Maintenance* (1996) and P. Reddin, *Dealing with Disrepair* (1996) – but is equally applicable to this book. Voluntary programmes – even those which intend and purport to go further than bare legal entitlement – will be vulnerable to legal challenge unless they also incorporate the legal minima. Of course, this is to state the difficulty – or the tension – in abstract and absolute terms: far more depends on practice and application; in truth, when a case comes to court, much turns on who will be able to assert the morally higher ground of reasonable conduct; none the less, no court, no matter how reasonable the landlord, will turn a blind eye to what is a clear breach of contract or other contravention of an individual's legal rights.

Which is where this Foreword came in: even though many of the legal *concepts* which are applicable to leasehold occupation are based on, if not (in part) identical to – certainly enjoy similarities with – those which are applicable to a tenancy (e.g. repairs and maintenance of structure of block or common parts, covenant for quiet enjoyment, nuisance, contractual provision of services), so that they should not pose great difficulties for the social housing manager: (a) there will be crucial differences "at the margins" of entitlement, with which the manager must be familiar; and, (b) what they mean in practice is likely to be very different in emphasis, especially when and if a matter proceeds to court.

The purpose of this book, therefore, is to help to equip the social landlord to perform one of the most *difficult* of all tasks: to keep a balance between the interests of tenants and of leaseholders; to be sure to provide leaseholders with no less than their legal rights, even when it is impracticable voluntarily to provide more to everyone – including the tenants; to understand and sympathetically to respond to disappointed expectations which may be common to others but which may now be enhanced by an investment in proprietorship; and, to recognise that the forms of contemporary social housing irreversibly include owner-occupation, which means in turn that the very same people who immediately beforehand needed support as tenants may now need it even more.

Andrew Arden QC
Arden Chambers
27 John Street
London WC1N 2BL

ARDEN

A

CHAMBERS

Table of Cases

Table of Statutes

Table of Statutory Instruments and Directions

Statutory Instruments

Directions

Abbreviations

HA	Housing Act
HAA 1985	Housing Associations Act 1985
HBCA 1984	Housing and Building Control Act 1984
HPA 1986	Housing and Planning Act 1986
LGHA 1989	Local Government and Housing Act 1989
LPA 1925	Law of Property Act 1925
LP(R)A 1938	Leasehold Property (Repairs) Act 1938
LRA 1967	Leasehold Reform Act 1967
LRHUDA 1993	Leasehold Reform, Housing and Urban Development Act 1993
LTA	Landlord and Tenant Act
LT(C)A 1995	Landlord and Tenant (Covenants) Act 1995
PEA 1977	Protection from Eviction Act 1977
RA 1977	Rent Act 1977

Introduction

Leaseholder management is a relatively recent discipline for social landlords. While housing associations for some time have had experience of shared ownership leaseholders, local authorities have seen the largest growth in leasehold stock as a result of right to buy since 1986. Housing associations now face a new wave of leasehold ownership through the right to acquire introduced by the Housing Act 1996. In this book, it will be seen that much of the correct approach to leaseholders applies equally to both housing associations and local authorities.

The management issues that arise are diverse. The most significant one is the dynamic relationship between the landlord's provision of services, repairs, maintenance, insurance and general management and the recovery of the costs for these from the leaseholder through the service charge. There is a strong element of supplier and consumer in this relationship. The larger part of this book is therefore devoted to this issue.

Leaseholders expect a good quality service, at the lowest possible cost, from the landlord. The quality of the service provided (sometimes by a third party) and the costs involved are key issues. Landlords seek to ensure that the services are of an acceptable quality and in many cases, to keep costs down, that the amount of time involved in management is tightly controlled. Given that the landlord and each of the leaseholders may have very different views as to quality of service/costs relationship, it will be appreciated how service charges can be a source of leaseholder ferment.

Problem areas

Service charges are as much an issue for social landlords as they are for private landlords. Both must efficiently monitor the services provided, collect the service charge and account for costs charged. For social landlords, with works contracts ranging across a number of buildings or estates, the only practical difference may be, on occasion, the greater burden of achieving the degree of precision in charging that is required.

Badly drafted leases and leaseholders' inability to pay charges are other problems common to both types of landlord.

There are however other issues which social landlords particularly must address. The problems that right to buy leaseholders have experienced are well documented. Many had no real appreciation before they purchased of the levels of charges for which they might be liable. As former secure tenants, many have found the charges for the repair or improvement of blocks not to be affordable. Indeed, these charges and the mixed tenure in many right to buy blocks have made right to buy flats difficult to sell, thereby locking in the leaseholders. Although recent measures in the Housing Act 1996 have been introduced with a view to alleviating these problems, right to buy leaseholders find themselves with these problems today. Hopefully, they will not be reproduced in the take up of right to acquire.

There is also the difficult question about the administration of leasehold management: Andrew Arden QC states in the Foreword to this book that leaseholders are 'a special breed, with special problems and special needs'. Social landlords must therefore consider how best to set up systems (whether specialised or as part of integrated housing management) that address and co-ordinate all aspects of leasehold management. Effective and efficient management depends on such organisation. This book seeks to highlight the management issues that must be addressed. Without consideration of these, management is 'vulnerable to disruption'.

Good practice

Understanding what has to be done

The starting point for every manager is familiarity with the lease itself. It sets out the minimum that is required of the landlord. Indeed, leaseholder's expectations arise primarily from its wording. As will appear, leases made between landlords and leaseholders differ in content from short term tenancies.

Additionally, statutory law provides leaseholders with rights independently of the terms of the lease. Familiarity with these rights is as essential as an understanding of the lease.

Beyond that there are a number of sources of regulation and guidance which should be complied with.

Communication with leaseholders

Good communication with leaseholders is an essential goal.

Leaseholders should be provided with as much information about future expenditure, changes in services or costs or other relevant matters as is sensibly possible. This helps them meet their own obligations under the service charge and often assists landlords in identifying mutually-acceptable arrangements. Likewise, their legitimate complaints (e.g. about the quality of services provided) help both with efficient management and pre-empting costly and time consuming resolution of disputes.

The provision of information for, and consultation with, leaseholders are now requirements of law in certain areas of leasehold management. Nevertheless, managers should not be deflected by the limited context of these legal requirements. Benefits are derived by managers from regular information exchange and consultation with leaseholders on all issues affecting them.

Monitoring the provision of services

If there is feedback from leaseholders, this may assist in ensuring that services provided are of acceptable quality. Nevertheless, there should, as part of the general system of leasehold management, be some on-going assessment of services by the landlord.

This assists in pre-empting disputes. Service charge disputes are often resolved in court by applying a test of reasonableness. Landlords, if challenged, need to be able to prove that the services, and costs, satisfy this test.

Long-term issues

Managers can pre-empt some problems that occur regularly. For leaseholders, the purchase process itself is an important point in time to establish management on the right track.

Notwithstanding legislative steps to provide leaseholders with estimates of the likely charges, it remains important to ensure that prospective leaseholders (e.g. under right to acquire) have as clear, and accurate, a view of the potential liabilities as possible.

Additionally, the way in which the lease terms are drafted and the way in which they work in practice for given buildings (or estates) should be monitored periodically. Information about defectively drafted leases should then be passed to the relevant conveyancing section.

Approach

This book approaches leaseholder management from the starting point of the relevant law. There is of course a range of steps that may be taken by managers that are not required by the legal rules (such as, fostering good relations with leaseholders or adopting simple billing techniques). But sight must never be lost of the fact that leaseholder disputes may ultimately have to be resolved in a court of law. It is a complicated legal area and therefore inevitably the larger part of this book sets out the detailed rules, the understanding of which is the foundation of good practice.

Layout of this book

Part I

The first chapter deals with the particular relationship of leaseholder and landlord. It compares short-term tenants and freeholders with leaseholders and then sets out the different types of leasehold that exist (e.g. right to buy or acquire and shared ownership). Chapter 2 explains the lease itself: how it works like a contract; the terms that commonly appear in all leases; and the typical terms that can be found in particular types of lease. It refers also briefly to the statutory and other regulatory sources relevant to leasehold management.

Part II

Chapter 3 is the first of five chapters that deal with the essential area of service charges. It describes how service charges work and details the way in which service charge clauses are commonly drafted in the lease. Further it draws a key distinction between annual charges and major works, leaving discussion of the latter until Chapter 5.

The important statutory provisions on service charges contained in the Landlord and Tenant Act 1985 are summarised in Chapter 4. In particular it deals: with the important reasonableness rule that underpins the whole topic; some of the requirements concerning information about service charges that leaseholders are entitled to; and the new jurisdiction under the Housing Act 1996 of leasehold valuation tribunals to adjudicate on service charge disputes. There is also a section on the way in which the total annual service charge should be calculated where individual cost items cannot be easily allocated to individual leaseholders.

Chapter 5 discusses major works, one of the most important topics for managers of leaseholders. It outlines the importance of: the provisions of the lease; informing leaseholders of likely charges arising from long-term major works projects; complying with the consultation procedure which must be followed prior to major works being carried out; and the efficient use of sinking funds to obtain funds in advance for such works.

The history of right to buy leases is explained in Chapter 6. Local authorities may need to deal with earlier versions of such leases and this chapter outlines some different features of earlier leases.

Chapter 7 focuses on the options available to a manager where service charges cannot be recovered from a leaseholder. If the leaseholder is simply unable to pay, the various forms of financial assistance available to leaseholders are set out. In particular, the new provisions for the reduction or waiver of service charge bills introduced by the Housing Act 1996 are discussed in detail. The manager's enforcement options are also set out.

Part III

Various other management issues are brought together in Chapter 8. Landlords' rights to improve a block of flats containing leaseholders, and the related problem of rights of access to carry out works, are considered here. The landlord's duties and rights in nuisance disputes between occupiers are also considered.

Where leases are badly drafted, it may be possible to obtain the agreement of the parties concerned to an appropriate variation of the terms. If not, an application may be possible for a variation of the lease by the court. The availability of such an application is also considered here.

There is now a range of ways in which leaseholders can monitor the way in which management is conducted. They may challenge a landlord's choice of insurer; obtain information, and make representations, about the appointment and employment of managing agents; require an audit in connection with the performance of the landlord's management obligations and the application of the service charge; and, as introduced by the Housing Act 1996, appoint a surveyor to advise on service charges. These are all discussed in Chapter 8.

Chapter 9 describes some of the principle ways in which the leaseholder's covenants in the lease can be enforced (remedies in connection with disrepair and nuisance are discussed in other titles in Arden's Housing Library). The main landlord's remedy is that of forfeiture. It constitutes a significant threat to a leaseholder. The procedure for exercising a forfeiture is described in detail. Suing for arrears of rent, insurance sums and/or service charge is also explained. Additionally, some particular remedies of leaseholders are outlined in brief.

The implications of assignment by the leaseholder and landlord are examined in Chapter 10. The enforceability of the covenants against the new assignee are considered here. The mortgage indemnity agreement and exchange sale schemes, introduced to help leaseholders sell their flats, are looked at in detail. Right to buy leaseholders' liability to repay some of the discount on assignment is dealt with in J. Henderson, *Rights to Buy and Acquire* (Arden's Housing Library) 1997.

Chapters 11 and 12 deal with various further matters that affect the security of leaseholders. Chapter 11 deals with what happens when a leasehold comes to its end. Chapter 12 deals with the rights (somewhat improved by the Housing Act 1996) of an individual leaseholder, or collectively with others, to buy an extension of the leasehold or the freehold of their house or flat.

Note that a list of abbreviations used (for titles of statutes etc.) appears at the beginning of the book and a glossary of technical terms starts on p.171.

Part I

1.
Leaseholders, Leaseholds and Leases

Who is a leaseholder? / Leaseholds and leases /
Other definitions / Types of leasehold

Who is a leaseholder?

Leaseholders and tenants

A 'leaseholder' (or 'lessee') commonly describes a person who owns a long lease (or leasehold) of a house or flat. By contrast, 'tenant' often describes a person in short-term residential accommodation. An assured tenant, secure tenant, protected tenant, statutory tenant or a person with a short-term tenancy who does not qualify as any of these is frequently called a 'tenant'.

The legal position of a leaseholder and a tenant at the most basic level is identical. Both leaseholder and tenant own a 'term of years absolute' (or lease) (section 1(1)(b) of the Law of Property Act (LPA) 1925), defined in section 205(1) (xxvii) of that Act to include both:

(a) arrangements of a fixed length (e.g. long leases); and
(b) periodic arrangements (short-term tenancies are commonly periodic, such as weekly tenancies).

Confusingly, the term 'leaseholder' does not appear in any of the legislation relevant to this subject. The only expression used to describe the owner of a term of years absolute is 'tenant', which thus includes the owner of a long lease.

Differences between leaseholders and tenants

Nevertheless a 'leaseholder' and 'tenant' as commonly understood are otherwise very different legal characters. A leaseholder takes a lease of significant fixed length (e.g. 100 years), whereas a tenant frequently has a weekly or monthly arrangement (excepting the scheme for assured shorthold tenants prior to the Housing Act 1996). The terms of a long lease are drafted in far greater detail than for a short-term arrangement. Historically there has been far more statutory regulation of short-term lettings. It is only in the last 20 years that there has been significant statutory intervention in the relationship between a leaseholder and his landlord. Before that, the parties were left principally to the terms set out in the lease. Most fundamentally, leaseholders are akin to freeholders in that the lease they own is effectively a capital asset, albeit a diminishing one, capable of disposal through, for example, sale or inheritance. By contrast tenants, notwithstanding the statutory protection of their security of tenure, have at most a (familial) right to occupy their premises indefinitely. This fundamental difference ultimately reflects the very different expectations that leaseholders have in connection with a landlord's management of the premises. Generally leaseholders require more efficient management and are more demanding than tenants.

Freeholders and leaseholders

Notwithstanding this close functional similarity between a leaseholder and freeholder, they own different types of property right and their legal positions are very different. All the advantages of freehold ownership are inaccessible to the purchaser of a flat. The reason for this relates to the historical development of land law in England and Wales. It is, in substance, not possible to bind successive owners of a freehold (of a house or flat) to carry out positive obligations (such as to repair or insure the building on their land). But restrictive covenants – which in essence require a landowner to desist from certain behaviour on his land – can in certain circumstances be enforced against successive owners of the freehold. Given then that the integrity of individual flats within a block is very much dependent on the integrity of the block as a whole, if each flat is owned in freehold it is not possible to guarantee that the block as a whole can be kept in a proper state of repair, or satisfactorily insured against destruction, in whole or part. The term of years absolute (or lease) provides a legal mechanism to enforce such positive covenants (i.e. by the landlord against each flat's leaseholder). Accordingly, all flats owners today own leaseholds of their flats.

Recent legislation permits leaseholders to buy their landlord's interest in their flat and thereby obtain control of the freehold (see Chapter 12 below). However, this legislation still results in the leaseholder owning both a leasehold of the flat and, at the same time, a controlling stake in the freehold ownership and, therefore, the landlord management of the block.

In this book, save where there is direct quotation from statutory materials or where the context otherwise requires, the owner of a long lease in a flat is referred to as a 'leaseholder'.

Leaseholds and leases

As stated above, 'lease' means precisely the same as the technical term 'term of years absolute'. Further, 'tenancy' and 'leasehold' also mean exactly the same. All four terms mean the property right which entitles its owner to exclusive possession of certain property for a fixed maximum duration (i.e. the property right recognised in section 1(1)(b) of LPA 1925).

In the legislation relevant to this subject, 'tenancy' and 'lease' are predominantly used to describe this property right. In this book, however, save where there is direct quotation from statutory materials or where the context otherwise requires, the property right owned by a leaseholder is referred to as the 'leasehold'. More particularly, 'leasehold' is used to describe long leaseholds rather than short-term letting arrangements.

'Lease' is also (quite properly) used to describe the document which creates the leasehold and contains all the terms agreed between the original landlord and the original leaseholder. In this work, save where there is direct quotation from statutory materials or where the context otherwise requires, 'lease' is therefore used to refer to the document.

Other definitions

All leaseholds are created out of a property right that is greater in extent and/or duration than themselves. This greater property right may be the freehold in the flat or may itself be a leasehold interest. During the course of the leasehold the owner of the freehold or 'superior' leasehold has rights and duties in relation to the flat albeit that he or she is not entitled to exclusive possession of it. Once the leasehold comes to an end, that owner is then entitled to exclusive possession. Until that day, the bundle of rights vested in the superior owner is called the 'reversion'. The reversion may also be defined as the right to exclusive possession of the property consequent upon the coming to an end of the leasehold.

The 'landlord' (or 'lessor') is the person or organisation who owns the reversion.

Types of leasehold

Leaseholds vary considerably in length. A fixed term of any significant length is a leasehold for the purposes of the distinction discussed above. However most of the relevant legislation applies where there is a term of years absolute of more than 21 years. Certain unusual long leaseholds are treated as exceeding 21 years in duration.

Social landlords are unlikely to come across leaseholds of less than 21 years. Their leaseholders will have acquired leaseholds in a variety of ways; these are discussed below by reference to the types of social landlord that exist.

Unusual long leaseholds

The duration of leaseholds which are defined so that they terminate on a person's death or marriage is converted into a fixed duration of 90 years (section 149(6) of LPA 1925). A perpetually renewable leasehold (i.e. a leasehold that contains a covenant enabling the leaseholder to renew it again and again) is converted into a leasehold with a fixed duration of 2,000 years (section 145 of LPA 1925). Both these leaseholds are unusual in the social rented sector.

Local authorities

Right to buy

A secure tenant is entitled to buy a leasehold (at a discount-ed price) where his or her dwelling-house is a flat whether or not his or her landlord owns the freehold (section 118(1)(b) of the Housing Act (HA) 1985). For the meaning of 'secure tenant', see A. Dymond, *Security of Tenure* (Arden's Housing Library) 1995. The length of the leasehold to which the secure tenant is entitled depends on the circumstances. If the landlord is a freeholder, or owns a leasehold of which not less than 125 years and five days are unexpired, the entitle-ment is to a leasehold for a term of not less than 125 years (section 139 and Schedule 6, paragraph 12(1) of HA 1985). In any other case, the entitlement is to a leasehold expiring five days before the term of the landlord's leasehold of the dwelling-house (Schedule 6, paragraph 12(2)). If the landlord has, since 8 August 1980, already granted a leasehold under the above provisions to a secure tenant within a block of flats, then subsequent flat owners exercising their right to buy may, at the landlord's discretion, be granted a leasehold which matches the term of the other leasehold or leaseholds (Schedule 6, paragraph 12(3)). This provision promotes a degree of efficiency in the block's management.

Additionally, the leasehold must be granted at a rent not exceeding £10 per annum (Schedule 6, paragraph 11).

For fuller consideration of the right to buy, see J. Henderson, *Rights to Buy and Acquire* (Arden's Housing Library) 1997.

Right to acquire on rent to mortgage terms

To assist a secure tenant who wishes to exercise his or her right to buy but who is unable to afford the full purchase price, the Leasehold Reform, Housing and Urban Development Act (LRHUDA) 1993 (see section 143 of HA 1985) permits a (secure) tenant, since 11 October 1993, to acquire a leasehold on 'rent to mortgage terms'. In outline this scheme allows the secure tenant to pay part of the right to buy leasehold value in the flat – the balance of the purchase price remaining unpaid. That part payment is funded by a mortgage which the (now) leaseholder pays off using the same sums as were formerly paid as rent to the landlord. The leaseholder thus owns the leasehold in part and makes mortgage payments for that part. The remaining equity in the leasehold is owned by the landlord (being protected as a second charge against the leasehold). This remaining equity either can be bought by the leaseholder by making further voluntary payments to the landlord, or must be paid off upon a disposal of the leasehold or the leaseholder's death.

The length of the leasehold to which the tenant is entitled and the rent payable are the same as for an ordinary right to buy leasehold (section 151 of and Schedule 6, paragraphs 11 and 12 to HA 1985). For fuller consideration of rent to mortgage, see J. Henderson, *Rights to Buy and Acquire* (Arden's Housing Library) 1997, Ch. 9.

Right to shared ownership

Before the introduction of rent to mortgage in 1993, legislative encouragement to secure tenants unable to afford to exercise their right to buy was introduced by the Housing and Building Control Act (HBCA) 1984 in the form of the 'shared ownership' leasehold (section 143 of HA 1985, now substituted). By this device, the secure tenant again purchased, by mortgage if necessary, a proportion of the flat's capital value on long leasehold (being a 50 per cent share at the minimum). Additionally, the (now) leaseholder paid a rent to the landlord for the remainder of the capital value. Together the monthly repayments on any mortgage and the additional rent payments would be less than full mortgage repayments. If the leaseholder wished to buy further shares in the flat's equity (in tranches of 12.5 per cent or multiples of that figure – a process known as 'staircasing') that option would be provided for in the lease.

The length of the leasehold to which he or she was entitled was the same as for the right to buy leasehold (section 151 (now substituted) of and Schedule 6, paragraphs 11 and 12 to HA 1985). The rent payable, prior to ownership of 100 per cent of the leasehold (when the rent would be not more than £10 per annum) was calculated by reference to a specific formula (section 151 (now substituted) of, and Schedule 6, paragraph 11 and Schedule 8, paragraph 4 (now repealed) to HA 1985).

Shared ownership did not prove popular and was withdrawn (section 107(c) of LRHUDA 1993).

Voluntary sales

Local authorities have power to dispose of their housing stock by way of general sale (section 32 of HA 1985). Under this power, local authorities have voluntarily created a number of ordinary and shared ownership leaseholds of flats.

Housing associations

Right to buy and right to shared ownership leaseholds

Prior to HA 1988, substantial numbers of housing association tenants were secure tenants because many housing associations were bodies which satisfied the 'landlord condition' under section 80 of HA 1985. Subject to the exclusion of secure tenants of certain housing associations (by section 120 of and Schedule 5 to HA 1985), these secure tenants were entitled to exercise the right to buy and right to a shared ownership leasehold in precisely the same way as local authority secure tenants (see J. Henderson, *Rights to Buy and Acquire* (Arden's Housing Library) 1997).

The Housing Act 1988 implemented a policy shift that new tenants of housing associations were to be treated as assured tenants within the rules of the private sector. Such tenants therefore cannot now qualify as secure tenants within the right to buy provisions of HA 1985. However, as a result of a number of exceptions and savings under HA 1988, there are still some secure tenants of housing associations who may be able to exercise the right to buy (or on rent to mortgage terms) in precisely the same way as local authority secure tenants (see above).

Preserved right to buy

A large amount of local authority property rented by secure tenants has now been transferred to private landlords and, in particular, housing associations. Such transfers bring a secure tenancy to an end in most circumstances (see section 80 of HA 1985). However, by sections 171A and 171B of HA 1985, where a person ceases to be a secure tenant because the landlord disposes of its interest in the flat (i.e. the landlord's reversion) to a person who is not a body within section 80 of HA 1985, the former secure tenant retains a 'preserved right to buy' so long as he or she occupies the flat as his or her only or principal dwelling-house. For a full discussion see J. Henderson, *Rights to Buy and Acquire* (Arden's Housing Library) 1997.

Again the tenant is entitled to exercise the right to buy in the same way as a secure tenant subject to certain modifications (made by the Housing (Preservation of Right to Buy) Regulations 1993 (SI No 2241 – see Chapter 2). However, notably, the new landlord is not given the power to match the term of the lease granted to the terms of other flats in the building. Further, there is no right to acquire on rent to mortgage terms.

Shared ownership

Housing associations (and local authorities) have been developing shared ownership leaseholds since the late 1970s. Therefore discussion of shared ownership here is not confined to the specific right to a shared ownership leasehold given under section 143 of HA 1985 (as it then was). Under this heading are considered shared ownership leaseholds which, although similar in nature to section 143 shared ownership leaseholds, are granted under housing associations' general powers to grant fixed term leaseholds.

By section 106 of the Housing Associations Act (HAA) 1985, a shared ownership leasehold means one:

(a) granted on payment of a premium calculated on a percentage of the flat's value or the cost of providing it; or

(b) under which the leaseholder (or personal representative) is or may be entitled to a sum calculated, directly or indirectly, on the flat's value.

Item (a) reflects the nature of most shared ownership schemes as previously discussed (i.e. the leaseholder initially buys only a share in the flat). 'Staircasing', although very

common today, is not an essential feature of shared ownership. Item (b) covers those schemes under which the leaseholder might relinquish the leasehold for compensation from
the landlord (e.g. when the leaseholder wants to sell the
leasehold, the landlord has a right to purchase the leaseholder's share for its full value).

Where the shared ownership scheme is HAG funded,
the minimum term of the leasehold must be 25 years longer
than the term of the association's loan. Otherwise there is no
fixed rule. Sample leases, issued by the Housing Corporation
and Housing for Wales, lay down a term for the leasehold of
99 years. Rent is dealt with by a specific formula and is calculated to meet the association's loan requirements.

Leasehold schemes for the elderly

Housing associations and some private landlords have
developed a number of leasehold schemes for the elderly.
Section 4 of HBCA 1984 defines a flat within such a scheme
as one which:

1. is of a number of flats which are particularly suitable
   for pensioners because of their location, size, design,
   heating system and other features;
2. the landlord lets to pensioners (and to physically disabled persons);
3. and has special facilities including the services of:
   (a) a resident warden; or
   (b) a non-resident warden, a system for calling him
       and the use of a common room in close proximity
       to the flat.

These schemes may be framed in different ways. Some
schemes involve the creation of ordinary long leaseholds
with the leaseholders paying a low or nominal rent. Other
schemes are in substance shared ownership schemes. The
distinguishing features of these schemes are the provision of
the services of a warden and, because the flats are particu-

larly suitable for the elderly, the leaseholder's right of alienation is restricted to keep the leasehold within the ownership of an elderly person.

The most recent Housing Corporation draft leasehold for the elderly (1989) is of the shared ownership variety. Similar to the sample shared ownership lease, it lays down a term for the leasehold of 99 years and the rent is dealt with by a specific formula.

Right to acquire under HA 1996

The HA 1996 now extends the right to buy to tenants of housing associations who were previously outside the provisions of HA 1985. For full consideration of the new provisions, see J. Henderson, *Rights to Buy and Acquire* (Arden's Housing Library) 1997.

Private landlords

Leaseholders of private landlords are unlikely to hold their flat under any of the distinct leasehold types discussed above. As with leaseholds generated in voluntary sales, they are of infinite variety, although most will conform to the general pattern of covenants (e.g. repair, insurance and service charges) found in all leaseholds.

Financing

Leaseholds held of a local authority property, whether effected under the right to buy provisions, or by way of voluntary sales, are often supported by a mortgage, usually of a building society. Formerly, a right to buy secure tenant had a right to be granted a mortgage from the local authority in aid of his or her purchase of the leasehold. This right was withdrawn (section 107(a) of LRHUDA 1993). Under the new rent to mortgage scheme the leaseholder pays sums (formerly paid as rent to the local authority) as mortgage payments to a building society.

Additional powers of local authorities in connection with mortgages are considered in Chapter 10.

Private financing is likely to be sought by a tenant exercising the right to buy or right to acquire against a housing association. Thus a mortgagee is likely to be involved in the purchase of a shared ownership leasehold. Leasehold schemes for the elderly may or may not involve mortgage support. It is a feature of these schemes that the leaseholder will sometimes have acquired enough capital to purchase the leasehold unaided.

The introduction of voluntary purchase grants in 1996 allows tenants to purchase their flats from associations participating within the scheme.

Key points

- Leaseholders own much longer leaseholds than short term residential tenants. They are not regulated by the statutory provisions that apply to regulated, assured and secure tenants.
- Leaseholders' rights and expectations are similar to those of freehold owners of land. Statutory rules, in certain circumstances, provide leaseholders with the opportunity to buy the freehold owned by their landlord.
- Every leaseholder will possess a lease (the document which creates a leasehold) which relates to their leasehold.
- Individual leaseholds differ as to: their length; the terms in the lease; the statutory rules that apply to them; and, as to the circumstances in which they were created.
- For social landlords, the commonest types of leasehold will be the 'right to buy' and 'shared ownership' leaseholds.
- The 'right to buy' leasehold is one purchased by a former tenant of a social landlord and owned in its entirety by the leaseholder. Examples are: the ordinary type; the 'rent to mortgage' type; and the new 'right to acquire' type.

- The 'shared ownership' leasehold is one owned in part by the leaseholder and in part by the social landlord. The leaseholder will often pay mortgage sums to a mortgagee in connection with the part purchased and rent to the social landlord in connection with the part not purchased.

2.
The Legal Framework

Express covenants / Implied covenants /
Covenants in local authority leases /
Covenants in housing association leases /
Statutory regulation and guidance

The lease is the starting point for every leasehold problem.
Leaseholds for a term of more than three years must be
created by deed (sections 52 and 54(2) of LPA 1925). The
lease is the formal document which gives effect to the full
creation of the leasehold and satisfies this legal rule.

This formality serves to record the various rights and
obligations (the 'terms' or 'covenants' of the lease) that each
original party to the lease agrees should bind the leasehold
and the reversion. This record is essential because these
terms, unless varied, bind not only the original parties, but
all subsequent owners of the leasehold and the reversion.
Exceptionally, where expressly agreed covenants do not cover a given situation, it is possible to imply a covenant into the
lease that deals with the point (see below). Alternatively, it
may be possible to effect an appropriate variation of the lease
(see Chapter 8).

Express covenants

Leases are usually lengthy and detailed, with a lot of cross-
referencing of covenants. Always read the whole lease before

trying to apply any of its particular covenants. The actual wording (of covenants) needs to be looked at closely. Most leases have a fairly standard structure as there are common types of covenant which deal with the usual problems of leasehold management. So it is worth becoming familiar with this structure.

Subject to specific types of leasehold (see Chapter 1), common items/covenants within a lease include the following:

The demise

Fundamentally, all leases must contain words that effect a grant by the landlord to the leaseholder.

The Particulars

This is the introductory section. It includes the Land Registry details and the Particulars. The Particulars are sometimes helpfully displayed in box form. Otherwise they are found in the opening clauses of the lease. They include:

- the lease date; the names of the original leaseholder and landlord (the landlord's address should be included (section 48 of LTA 1987) – see Chapter 9);
- the property (i.e. the definition of the plot of land upon which the building containing the flat is situated);
- the premises (i.e. the flat);
- the premium (probably the most important part of the consideration for granting the leasehold, which includes the rent and the leaseholder's other covenants);
- the rent (a nominal 'ground' rent, though not essential, is often included; there may even be a rent review clause);
- the term, i.e. the commencement date and the length of the leasehold; and
- the leaseholder's share of the annual service charge.

Definitions

Most leases contain a definition section to assist the reader. In particular, there should be a definition of the building containing the flat and the estate or wider environment with which the building is connected functionally. There may also be a definition of the common parts of the building.

The definition of the leaseholder's flat may stipulate that the entirety of the floor of the flat belongs to the leaseholder (i.e. right through to the flat below). On the other hand, it may only bring the top half of the floor within the flat. Alternatively, it may exclude specific items (e.g. main girders) from the floor.

Included rights

The leaseholder is granted additional rights for the flat's proper use, usually in a schedule to the lease. They include access over common parts of the building and footpaths and driveways; passage for services through pipes and cables in other parts of the building or estate and access to maintain them; support and protection from other parts of the building and access to those parts to protect or maintain the flat; the benefit of covenants entered into by other flat owners with the landlord (this allows the leaseholder to enforce positive and restrictive covenants against original leaseholders of other flats, but not their successors; note that successors of other flat owners may be bound by restrictive covenants where a 'letting scheme' has been specifically created, see below and Chapter 8); and other minor rights such as the use of a dustbin.

Excepted rights

Certain rights, often detailed in a schedule, are usually reserved for the benefit of the landlord or the other flat owners within the block. They include passage for services through pipes and cables situated in the flat; support and protection provided by the flat for other parts of the building and access to it by other flat owners to protect or maintain their flats; access for the landlord to inspect or carry out his obligations (e.g. of repair) under the lease; the burden of covenants entered into by the landlord with any other flat owner; and the landlord's right to vary any 'regulations' affecting the block (see below).

More particularly, the landlord may reserve a right to alter or rebuild the building, and to alter the services provided.

Leaseholder's covenants

These include: to pay the rent, council tax and other outgoings; to repair and maintain the flat; to insure the flat; to redecorate the flat's interior; not to make any alteration to the flat's structure without the landlord's written consent; to permit the landlord access to inspect the state of, and to repair, the flat; not to sublet without the landlord's consent; to notify the landlord of any assignment or mortgage of the leasehold; and to pay any section 146 of LPA 1925 costs incurred by the landlord (see Chapter 9).

Further, the leaseholder will covenant to observe certain everyday restrictions, usually described as 'Regulations' and set out in a schedule to the lease. They bind the leaseholder not to do certain things, such as not to use the flat for any profession, trade, business, unlawful or immoral purpose; not to commit a nuisance; not to allow audible music to be played between certain hours; not to keep pets without the landlord's consent; and not to fix aerials to any part of the building.

Leaseholder's covenant to pay service charge or improvement contribution

The leaseholder will covenant to pay a service charge for specific 'services' provided by the landlord. These may be services which the landlord is specifically bound to provide (i.e. under the landlord's covenants – see below) or may be non-specific costs reasonably incurred by the landlord (provided in some leases as 'sweeper clauses').

The services provided may include redecoration, repair, cleaning, operation and maintenance of electrical and mechanical apparatus (e.g. lifts), providing rubbish disposal facilities, payment of charges etc., and insurance and general management.

The annual cost to the landlord of providing these services is likely to vary. Accordingly, given that each leaseholder pays a set share of the total annual cost of those services, each leaseholder's annual service charge correspondingly varies.

Commonly, the lease requires that an estimate will be made of the likely annual service charge for the forthcoming year. This estimate forms the basis for an advance payment (an 'interim charge') made, say, quarterly by the leaseholder. The interim charges and the actual costs total for the year then leave a balancing charge or credit. Every lease should set out in detail how the leaseholder's service charge is to be calculated and paid (see further, Chapter 3).

Landlord's covenants

These may include: to require other flat owners to enter into subsequent leases containing similar covenants to those in the leaseholder's own lease for the mutual benefit of all the flat owners (so as to create a letting scheme under which leaseholders can enforce restrictive – not positive – covenants against each other); to keep the main structure, pipes etc., common parts and installations enjoyed in common with other leaseholders in repair; to provide cleaning and other services; to insure the building (and to repair or rebuild the building where damaged or destroyed with the insurance monies); to give the leaseholder quiet enjoyment of the flat; and, upon being indemnified as to costs, to enforce covenants against any other defaulting flat owner within the building.

Forfeiture

The landlord's right to forfeit the leasehold following breach of any of the leaseholder's covenants is always included.

Implied covenants

Common law

Where a lease is defective, ambiguous or silent on a matter it is possible at common law to imply covenants between the parties.

The courts have used two approaches. First, they do so on the basis of specific facts. Here the courts must be satisfied that both parties would have agreed to the term at the time of the agreement: this is known as the 'business efficacy test'. Secondly, they may imply a covenant as a matter of law. Here one of the accepted justifications for implying a term is that the contract is of a defined type and implicitly requires the term.

> **Case report**
>
> **The House of Lords held that where an essential means of access to units in a building in multiple occupation is retained in the landlord's control, there is an implied obligation on the landlord's part to take reasonable care to keep it in reasonable repair and usability.** *Liverpool City Council v Irwin* **(1977). (See also, for example,** *Barnes v City of London Real Property Company* **and** *Finchbourne v Rodriguez* **in Chapter 3.)**

Statute

A small number of statutory rules imply covenants into long leaseholds. These are dealt with below.

Covenants in local authority leases

Right to buy lease

A right to buy lease must contain certain covenants. (For full consideration of the terms of right to buy leasehold, see J. Henderson, *Rights to Buy and Acquire* (Arden's Housing Library) 1997, Ch. 6.) Note that the law has changed on a number of occasions and leases granted in the early 1980s may be different (see Chapter 6).

The most significant covenants usually included are as follows.

Repayment of discount

The leaseholder must repay the discount received on purchase if there is a 'relevant disposal' of the flat within three years of the grant of the leasehold (section 155 of HA 1985).

Repair and maintenance (landlord)

Subject to court sanctioned agreement to the contrary, the landlord must repair and/or maintain the structure and exterior of the flat and building (see Chapter 6); other property used by the leaseholder; and the services provided to the tenant and the installations providing those services. The landlord must also rebuild and re-instate the dwelling-house if destroyed (Schedule 6, paragraph 14 to HA 1985). But there is no obligation on either party to insure; insurance is dealt with in individual leases according to the landlord's preference.

Interior repair

The leaseholder, unless agreed to the contrary, must keep the flat's interior in repair, including decorative repair (Schedule 6, paragraph 16).

Service charges

The leaseholder may have to make a reasonable contribution to the costs incurred by the landlord carrying out the above implied covenants. This contribution is limited during an initial period (see Schedule 6, paragraphs 16A *et seq* to HA 1985 and Chapter 6). After that initial period the lease-holder is bound by the general covenant to pay service charges. This covenant is not required by HA 1985 to be framed in any particular form.

Costs of improvement

The landlord may include a covenant requiring the lease-holder to contribute to any improvements effected by the landlord (although this is restricted during an initial period – see Chapter 6). Coupled with contemplated future improvement of the building, the landlord may reserve the right to make alterations and/or improvements to it.

Prohibited covenants

Note that a covenant which:
1. prohibits assignment or subletting, in whole or in part;
2. purports to charge the leaseholder for giving a consent; or
3. is in the circumstances unreasonable is prohibited (Schedule 6, paragraphs 17, 6 and 5).

Conclusion

Save for the mandatory covenants, right to buy leases can (and do) exhibit considerable variety in the way that they are drafted. Note that a right to buy lease should not include a covenant by the landlord to require other flat owners to enter into subsequent leases containing similar covenants to those in the leaseholder's own lease. To do so would require a landlord to include inappropriate Housing Act 1985 covenants (e.g. as to repayment of discount) into all sub-sequent leases whether they were right to buy leases or not and whether or not the terms of the voluntary disposal consent include a discount payment clause.

Rent to mortgage lease

Rent to mortgage leases must follow the requirements laid down for right to buy leases. (For full consideration of the terms of rent to mortgage leasehold, see J. Henderson, *Rights to Buy and Acquire* (Arden's Housing Library) 1997, Ch. 9.) Particular covenants must be included in the rent to mortgage lease, as follows.

Final payment of landlord's equity share

The leaseholder must pay off the landlord's share in the equity if there is a relevant disposal or a relevant death (section 151A of and Schedule 6A, paragraph 1 to HA 1985).

Interim or final payments to redeem landlord's share

The leaseholder is entitled to make interim payments or a final payment, in redemption of the landlord's share, at any time (section 151A of and Schedule 6A, paragraph 2 to HA 1985). Terms concerned with valuations associated with interim or final payment are also provided for.

Service charges

In line with the leaseholder's partial ownership of the lease-hold, his or her liability to pay service charges and/or improvement contributions is restricted to the extent of his or her ownership of the equity (section 151 of and Schedule 6, paragraph 16E to HA 1985). If the leaseholder owns 60 per cent of the equity, he or she is bound only to pay 60 per cent of the charge or contribution that he or she would otherwise have been required to pay.

Right to shared ownership lease

The shared ownership lease was modelled closely on the right to buy lease and, save for those covenants particular to it (see Schedule 8 to HA 1985 (now repealed) for the comprehensive terms), contained the same covenants as the right to buy lease (section 151 of HA 1985 (now substituted)).

Particular covenants usually included are:

- a note of the leaseholder's initial share (Schedule 8, paragraph 1 to HA 1985);
- the option to acquire further shares in the equity (Schedule 8, paragraph 1);
- a term dealing with the computation of the rent payable by the leaseholder prior to acquisition of 100 per cent of the equity (Schedule 8, paragraph 4);
- for the leaseholder to repay the discount received on purchase if there is a 'relevant disposal' of the flat within five years of the grant of the leasehold (section 155 (now substituted));
- for the leaseholder to pay to the landlord any outstanding share if there is a 'relevant disposal' of the flat before the leaseholder owns 100 per cent of the equity (Schedule 8, paragraph 6);
- a term prohibiting a disposal of part of the flat before the leaseholder owns 100 per cent of the equity (Schedule 8, paragraph 9).

Indeed, save for the covenants required by statute, shared ownership leases also have exhibited considerable variety in the covenants.

Covenants in housing association leases

Right to buy and right to shared ownership leases

The terms of these leases are the same as for local authority granted leases, above.

Preserved right to buy

The preserved right to buy lease is modelled closely on the right to buy lease and, save for specific modifications (see the Housing (Preservation of Right to Buy) Regulations 1993 (SI No 2241)), contains the same covenants (section 171C of HA 1985).

Particular modifications of note are as follows:
- there must be a statement that the grant of the lease was made under the preserved right to buy provisions (Schedule 9A, paragraph 7(1) of HA 1985);
- the new landlord has discretion whether to include a covenant to repay the discount in the lease; if such a covenant is inserted it must not be more onerous than that prescribed by section 155 of HA 1985.

Shared ownership

The Housing Corporation and Housing for Wales produce sample shared ownership leases. Different versions of these samples have been issued in the past. They do not have to be used but there are certain clauses that must always be included.

Rent payable

■ A 'rent review' clause computes the rent payable by the leaseholder prior to 100 per cent acquisition of the equity.

Option to acquire further shares

A leaseholder may acquire further shares in the equity. In grant funded schemes the minimum initial share of the equity purchased must be 25 per cent. Further, the right to staircase to 100 per cent must be effected in four steps.

Transfer of leasehold by leaseholder

Such provisions might require the leaseholder to staircase to 100 per cent and then transfer the leasehold at full value. Alternatively, the leaseholder might be required to sell to a purchaser nominated by the landlord for a consideration that is no greater than the leaseholder's share in the equity. Certain types of transfer are exempt from these provisions (e.g. transfer on death).

Mortgage protection

This clause may allow a mortgagee to offer to surrender the leasehold to the landlord for a set figure and/or entitle the mortgagee to complete the staircasing to 100 per cent and then sell the leasehold. This clause assists the mortgagee in the protection and realisation of the security.

Variation of terms

In registered land, there will be a clause providing for a restriction to be entered preventing any variation of the lease terms without the Housing Corporation's consent.

Other clauses

The Housing Corporation requires a set clause concerning stamp duty. Housing for Wales requires an absolute covenant against alterations of the flat's structure and exterior; a covenant not to alter the flat's interior without consent; a covenant not to deal in any way with part only of the flat; and a covenant not to sublet the whole of the flat.

Leasehold schemes for the elderly

The Housing Corporation and Housing for Wales produce sample leases based on the shared ownership model. These samples do not have to be used but there are certain clauses that should always be included.

Assignment

Assignment is prohibited to anyone under age 55. The landlord may retain a right to nominate a purchaser. In the shared ownership style leasehold, there is a term requiring the leaseholder to sell to a purchaser for a consideration that is no greater than the leaseholder's share in the equity.

To emphasise the policy of preserving the benefits of these leasehold schemes for the elderly, there may be a term prohibiting occupation of the flat by a person under age 55 (excepting the leaseholder's spouse).

Subletting

Subletting the whole or part of the premises is prohibited.

Warden

The landlord must provide the leaseholder with the services of, and a system for calling, a warden. Although not prescribed, such services should be set out in careful detail.

Other comments

In shared ownership style leaseholds, there are included terms dealing with the computation of rent payable by the leaseholder prior to 100 per cent acquisition of the equity, and the leaseholder's option to acquire further shares in the equity. The Housing Corporation also requires the afore-mentioned mortgagee protection clause and terms dealing with the restriction against variation and stamp duty.

Right to acquire under HA 1996

For full consideration of the new provisions see J. Henderson, *Rights to Buy and Acquire* (Arden's Housing Library) 1997.

Private landlords

The covenants usually included by private landlords have evolved over time into what are now familiar express covenants (see the examples outlined above). Several obvious points nevertheless may be made.

First, the legal rules enabling the landlord to enforce repairing covenants against a leaseholder are not particularly effective. Accordingly, it is common for the landlord to have the responsibility (and right) to effect important repairs (i.e. to the structure). Secondly, given the importance to the landlord (as well as the leaseholder) that the building is properly insured, it is administratively much more efficient for the landlord to insure the building as a whole. This is the common approach for landlords of blocks of flats.

Statutory regulation and guidance

The starting point for any management problem involves the housing manager turning to the lease terms – a necessary but

not the only step. After the relevant lease terms are identified, further consideration must be given to two other
matters: first, whether the issue is additionally governed by
particular statutory rules; and, secondly, (whether statutory
rules are relevant or not) whether due weight must given to
relevant code of practice or guidance.

Statutory law

The principal leasehold management legislation is contained
in the recent Landlord and Tenant Acts and Housing Acts.
These are dealt with in detail later in this book. This legislation was designed to protect the (private) leaseholder and
lays down rules providing the leaseholder with civil law
rights. Certain statutory rules provide that failure to comply
with a relevant rule is a criminal offence.

Codes of practice and guidance

Section 87 of LRHUDA 1993

This section provides that the Secretary of State may approve
any code of practice which appears to him to be designed to
promote desirable practices in any matter(s) directly or indirectly concerned with the management of residential property by landlords or their managing agents. While non-compliance with such a code of practice does not in itself provide
a leaseholder with a remedy in civil law, in any court or tribunal proceedings the code is admissible as evidence, and
any relevant part of the code is taken into account to determine the issue in dispute. Statutory law introduces the all
important concept of reasonableness into service charge disputes. Accordingly, section 87 codes have a significant ancil-
lary role to play in the outcome of these disputes.

The Association of Retirement Housing Managers has
drawn up a code of practice that has now been approved by
the Secretary of State (the Approval of Codes of

Management Practices (Residential Property) (No 2) Order 1995 (SI No 3149) bringing the code into force on 1 January 1996). This code applies to schemes which are specifically designed and designated for retired older people. It is therefore of significant relevance to housing associations running such schemes.

The Royal Institute of Chartered Surveyors has prepared a code entitled 'Service charge: Residential Management Code' that has been approved by the Secretary of State and is in force from 17 March 1997. The code applies to properties where a service charge, which varies according to the expenditure, is payable and the landlord is not a public sector landlord or registered housing association.

Sections 36A of HAA 1985 and 36 of HA 1996

Section 36A of HAA 1985 empowered the Housing Corporation and Housing for Wales to issue guidance on the management of housing accommodation by registered housing associations. In considering whether action was needed under the HAA 1985 against an association to secure the proper management of an association's affairs or whether there had been mismanagement, the extent to which such guidance was being followed was a relevant consideration.

Both the Housing Corporation and Housing for Wales issued guidance under this power entitled 'The Leaseholder's Guarantee'. This power to issue guidance is now re-enacted by section 36 of HA 1996. As before, compliance with any guidance issued is relevant when considering whether action under Schedule 1 of HA 1996 needs to be taken against an association.

Other guidance

The Department of Environment has issued guidance to local authorities entitled 'A guide to good practice on the administration of service charges and improvement contributions'.

Key points

- Always start with the lease. It operates like a contract setting out the rights and duties that bind the leaseholder and landlord.
- The terms of the lease should deal with the common problems in leasehold management. If not, it may be possible exceptionally to imply terms into, or vary the terms of, the lease.
- Certain common matters are usually covered in the lease. Importantly, there will be: the service, maintenance, repair and insurance obligation imposed on the landlord ; and, the obligation imposed on the leaseholder to pay for those matters ('the service charge').
- A 'right to buy' lease contains particular covenants for the repayment of the discount received on purchase and restrictions on the service charges and improvement contributions payable in the early years of the leasehold.
- The 'shared ownership' lease contains particular covenants concerned with: rent review; the purchase of further shares; assignment; and, mortgagee protection.
- Leasehold schemes for the elderly are characterised by covenants for the provision of a warden and prohibiting assignment to persons under age 55.
- After the lease, consider the statutory law (dealt with from Chapter 4 onwards). Lastly, a number of codes of practice deal with certain management matters. Their good practice should be followed.

Part II

3.
Service Charge

Annual charges and major works compared /
The lease

The primary concern of the landlord manager is to ensure that the building is properly maintained and insured, thereby protecting its value. The leaseholder has identical concerns but more widely expects to be provided with such services and maintenance of facilities as are provided for in the lease. All these matters should therefore be comprehensively dealt with in the lease. Invariably, the landlord is responsible under the covenants in the lease for all or most of these matters. This imposes on the landlord a significant management burden: responsibility not only for organising repairs, insurance, services for the leaseholders and any relevant maintenance (referred to hereafter generally as 'services') but also for incurring the costs of providing these services.

Chapter 2 shows that through the service charge clause, service and management costs are always passed on to the leaseholder. It is usually expected that landlords will not even have to fund initial management costs, let alone find themselves out of pocket. As a result there is normally a system for getting advance payment of service charges.

This chapter is the first of five chapters in Part II of the book that deals with the way the lease terms, the statutory law and relevant codes of practice and guidance shape the leasehold manager's approach to the question of service charges. The subject is considered in the following order:

- annual service charges (Chapters 3 and 4);
- major works (Chapter 5);
- right to buy leaseholds (Chapter 6); and,
- the recovery and enforcement of service charges (Chapter 7).

Annual charges and major works compared

Services of a recurring nature (such as small items of repair and maintenance, cleaning and caretaking, maintenance of communal parts and grounds, lighting, heating and hot water, lifts, entry phones/security and rubbish collection) are charged for each year ('annual charges'). Save for the precise cost, the charges will be anticipated by the leaseholders. The lease will detail the basis for calculating annual charges.

'Major works', by contrast, such as cyclical redecoration and large scale repair or improvement, occur less frequently and are more costly. Although no different to annual charges under the lease, they are treated somewhat differently under the statutory rules (see Chapter 5). But note that much of what is said in this chapter applies to major works.

The lease

As the contract between the parties, the lease defines what charges may be recovered from the leaseholder. If the lease operates in a way that is unfavourable to the leaseholder, the statutory law – which is designed to protect a leaseholder from unreasonable service charges – may apply to any dispute that arises. Additionally, subject to any variation of the lease (see Chapter 8), the terms may operate unfavourably against the landlord (i.e. by not providing for the recovery of an item of expenditure under the service charge clause). In all questions regarding recovery, the lease provisions must be assessed as an initial task before any question of statutory law or good practice arises.

Relationship of landlord's covenants to service charge clause

The landlord's covenants must be examined to identify those services which must be provided. The landlord has no discretion with these services and is obliged to perform the relevant covenants and may be forced to do so by any leaseholder who benefits from them. Where a clause provides that the leaseholder pays for certain services but the landlord is not expressly obliged to provide them, the court may imply an obligation upon the landlord to provide them (*Barnes v City of London Real Property Company* (1918).

The landlord may have discretion, rather than an obligation, to supply certain services. Check the lease for any specific or general provision (e.g. '... such services as he considers reasonable').

The landlord can only recover service charge costs (discretionary or obligatory) specified in the service charge clause.

> ### Case report
>
> **A landlord was obliged under covenants to carry out structural repairs to a building. However, because the service charge clause was poorly drafted, the leaseholder was not obliged to pay the cost of structural repairs carried out by the landlord. (Note that this might not be the outcome today – see below.) *Riverlate Properties Ltd v Paul* (1975).**

Courts will not remedy poor drafting by reading the lease in a way that ensures the landlord is not out of pocket (even though that is the reason a service charge clause is included). If the landlord provides discretionary or obligatory services that are not within the wording of the service charge clause, those costs cannot be recovered from the leaseholder. The only options then available to the landlord are to agree a variation of the lease with the leaseholder or by application to the court (see Chapter 8).

The obligation to provide services is strictly independent of the obligation to pay service charges (but see *Barnes v City of London Real Property Company* (1918), above). Non-payment of service charges does not entitle the landlord to withhold services from the leaseholder. Even where the provision of services is, under the lease terms, clearly dependent upon payment of service charges, the landlord needs to consider whether by withholding services this might constitute a criminal offence under section 1(3A) of the Protection from Eviction Act 1977.

Chargeable costs: generally

Methods of charging

Costs recoverable by the landlord through the service charge clause are commonly defined in one of two ways. First, they may be incurred by the landlord in performing the landlord's covenants. Here reference must be made to those covenants to identify which types of expenditure the landlord is obliged to incur. Only such expenditure is recoverable under the service charge.

Alternatively, without reference to those covenants, they may be incurred in connection with a list of chargeable items (which would appear in a schedule to the main body of the lease). The items may or may not fall within the landlord's covenants. This method permits the easy inclusion of discretionary services. In fact a single lease may contain both methods of charging by making a leaseholder liable not only for the cost to the landlord of complying with (some of) the landlord's covenants but also for the costs incurred by the landlord on scheduled items of expenditure.

Sweeper provisions

Limiting the chargeable items in the landlord's covenants or in the scheduled list risks excluding unanticipated items from the service charge clause. Thus a sweeper provision is often included that obliges or permits a landlord to provide a service that is considered reasonably necessary to manage the building properly (and in turn permits recovery of the cost). The provision's effectiveness depends entirely upon how it is worded; courts regard such clauses with caution. Before employing such a clause, the landlord should consider the risk of being unable to recover the expenditure from the leaseholder. The same applies to any provision which seeks to vary or add to the services the landlord is obliged to provide (note that such a variation provision may now be invalid under the Unfair Terms in Consumer Contracts Regulations 1994).

> **Case report**
>
> A landlord proposed to clean the walls of a building but was unable to specifically recover the costs of such work under the list of chargeable items. He attempted to recover the costs under the sweeper provision which allowed him 'to add, extend, vary or make any alteration in the rendering of the said service or any of them'. The court held that the landlord could not. The sweeper provision had to be read as only allowing the landlord to vary the existing types of service. Wall cleaning was a very different type of service to those that had been expressly set out in the lease. *Jacob Isbicki & Co Ltd v Goulding & Bird Ltd* (1989).

Particular chargeable costs

Service charge clauses commonly include the following important chargeable items.

Repairs and improvements

(For a detailed treatment of 'repair' see A. Kilpatrick, *Repairs and Maintenance* (Arden's Housing Library) 1996.)

In considering any issue of repair the following matters should be considered separately:

1. *The item of the building said to be in disrepair.* In considering the extent of the landlord's and leaseholder's covenants, the person responsible for the item of disrepair is identified. If the landlord effects repairs that are the leaseholder's responsibility, the cost cannot be recouped through the service charge, nor save where the landlord does the repair work by agreement with or at the request of the leaseholder, probably by any other means.

2. *Whether the item is suffering from any actual deterioration in its condition and, if so, whether it falls below the standard of maintenance required by the lease.* This decides whether the landlord is liable to carry out repairs.

3. *The work needed to repair the item to its proper condition required by the lease.* This covers short term (and less costly) repairs to more long term (and expensive) repairs. As a general rule, within the bounds of what repairs are legitimate, the party responsible for the repairs must choose which. Where the landlord chooses, this area is a potential source of disputes with leaseholders.

Case report

The landlords were responsible for repairing a block's window-frames. The leaseholders argued that the repairs should be effected piecemeal by attending only to any specifically rotted wood. The landlords proposed to replace all the window frames, a less expensive course in the long run. It was held that, under the covenant, the landlords were entitled to carry out the replacement work. *Reston Ltd v Hudson* (1990).

4. *Works beyond repair.* The courts, after much discussion of 'repair', have evolved a highly technical
approach to the question, in any given situation, of
what works amount to repair and what go beyond
repair (and which therefore fall outside an obligation
merely to repair). (See A. Kilpatrick, *Repairs and
Maintenance* (Arden's Housing Library) 1996, p. 25
et seq.) Work beyond repair is:
   (a) work that merely remedies an inherent defect in
       the building (where however the inherent defect
       causes disrepair within the meaning of 2. above,
       the position is different. If the only sensible way of
       curing the disrepair is also to remedy the inherent
       defect, then such remedial work amounts to repair);
   (b) work that effects a 'renewal' of the building as a
       whole; and,
   (c) work that constitutes an improvement of the
       building.

Where the landlord carries out works that may, in whole or
part, go beyond repair work but the service charge clause
covers only repair work, this may form the basis of a challenge by the leaseholder when the landlord seeks to recover
the costs through the service charge.

Case report

A landlord covenanted to 'repair' a block. It
replaced troublesome wood-framed windows with
wholly different and better double glazing windows and attempted to recover the costs from
the leaseholders. The court held that it could not
do so, and further was unable to do so under a
sweeper provision. *Mullaney v Maybourne Grange
(Croydon) Management Co Ltd* (1986).

Under **4.** above the wording of the landlord's covenant and
the service charge are all important. Some leases expressly
confer a right upon a landlord to effect works of 'renewal'

and/or 'improvement' which must be paid for by the lease-holder through the service charge. This is a particular feature of right to buy and right to acquire leases. As to improvement contributions, see Chapter 6.

Insurance

Building insurance should be provided for in the lease. If the landlord undertakes the obligation to insure, the leaseholder must re-imburse the landlord by paying an 'additional rent' towards the cost (see Chapter 9), or, by contributing through the service charge.

The service charge terms may permit a leaseholder to challenge paying the full insurance cost sought by the land-lord. A typical term might be that the leaseholder pays his or her share of 'the costs of and incidental to the performance by the landlord of his covenant to insure'. The wording may go further by providing that the insurance costs must be 'reasonable'. Under the strict terms of the lease, however, there is usually no implied obligation on the landlord that the insurance cost must be reasonable (*Bandar Property Holdings v Darwen* (1968).

> **Case report**
>
> Leaseholders challenged the amount charged for the full cost of insurance passed on by a local authority, notwithstanding that the authority had received a 25 per cent reduction from the insurers. The case report suggests that the 25 per cent reduction was provided by the insurers to cover the landlord's 'administration costs'. Several issues of principle were raised.
>
> First, insofar as the 25 per cent reduction was, in whole or part, a genuine attempt to rec-ompense the landlord for administration costs (e.g. surveying the buildings), it could be argued that, instead of passing on the 75 per cent figure plus an amount independently worked out for the

costs incurred in administering the insurance contract, the 100 per cent figure was the cost of and incidental to the performance of the covenant to insure. If however the 25 per cent reduction figure bore no real relation to the true administration costs, then it might be susceptible to challenge on the basis that it was not a true 'cost' of the insurance (or under section 19 of LTA 1985 – see below).

Secondly, however, if and to the extent that any part of the 25 per cent reduction was truly an inducement payment (a gratuity), then it is reasonably arguable that, again, it was not a 'cost' of the insurance. Accordingly, the benefit of any 'inducement' sum should be passed on to the leaseholder by taking account of it when computing the chargeable cost of the insurance.

Thirdly, other reductions of the *prima facie* cost of insuring buildings (e.g. discounts provided to landlords on block policies) may need to be reflected in the computation of the costs payable by the leaseholder. (Reported in *Inside Housing*, 25 August 1995)

For residential leaseholders the provisions of LTA 1985 are relevant (see Chapter 4). Other rights given to leaseholders in connection with building insurance and which may indirectly assist leaseholders in reducing such costs are considered in Chapter 8.

Professional fees

The service charge clause may cover 'the fees of managing agents' and/or 'the fees of professionals (e.g. solicitors, surveyors, accountants) whom the landlord reasonably employs in connection with the management and/or maintenance of the building'.

For private landlords the use of managing agents is an important topic. When appropriate, service charges ought properly to provide expressly for recouping managing agents' fees. If they do not, it is generally difficult to recoup such fees except where the costs relate purely to providing chargeable services. This subject is not dealt with in detail in this book because social landlords tend to manage their leasehold stock in-house (see below).

The fees of other professionals may be expressly within the service charge. Where there is no express provision, such fees may nevertheless be recoverable where incurred in providing services (including management services) by the landlord which are recoverable under the service charge (see *Plough Investments Ltd v Manchester City Council* (1989).

Where there is express provision, the fees chargeable must generally be incurred in connection with the leasehold management (see the example express term above to that effect). For example, legal fees charged to the leaseholders under the service charge must be seen to have been incurred in connection with management rather than for the landlord's benefit.

> **Case report**
>
> **A landlord was entitled to recover the fees of 'such other professional persons as may be necessary or desirable'. It was held that this clause did not entitle the landlord to recover the legal fees incurred in recovering arrears of rent and service charges from some of the leaseholders. *Sella House Ltd v Mears* (1989).**

In-house management

As with managing agents' fees, if in-house management costs are to be recovered that matter should be expressly provided for in the service charge. If it is not, it is unlikely that a court will allow recovery under the general wording of the clause (*Cleve House Properties v Schidlof* (1980). An application to court for variation of the lease to provide for such costs is likely to be ineffective (see Chapter 8).

In the absence of the clearest provision, a landlord cannot include an element of profit in the service charge. The charge in its ordinary function provides for reimbursement of expenditure and/or overheads (*Jollybird v Fairzone* (1990)).

Caretakers (including porters and wardens)

A lease may require or permit the landlord to provide a resident or non-resident caretaking *service* (without actually obliging the landlord to provide a designated caretaker). More commonly, the lease permits or requires the landlord to provide a resident or non-resident *caretaker*, in which case the caretaker's services should be set out in full.

Where a caretaking service, or a caretaker, is provided, the service charge clause should recoup the costs. These costs may include the caretaker's salary (in whole or part – see *Concorde Graphics v Andromeda Investments* (1983) and a notional rent for any accommodation provided for a resident caretaker (see *Lloyds Bank v Bowker Orford* (1992)).

Reasonableness of service charge

Service charge clauses commonly expressly include the word 'reasonable' in various connections. For instance, the clause may oblige a landlord 'to provide any service that he considers reasonably necessary for the proper management of the building', or require the leaseholder to pay a due share of 'the fees of professionals (e.g. solicitors, surveyors, accountants) whom the landlord reasonably employs in connection with the management and/or maintenance of the building'.

For the leaseholder's benefit, the charge may be limited to 'the reasonable cost' of the services provided, or to costs that are 'reasonably incurred' (see *Postel Properties Ltd v Boots* (1996)). Invariably a reasonableness provision is interpreted and applied according to the facts of each individual case, and generalisations cannot usefully be given about what is and is not reasonable. Ultimately the test is one of fairness. Including 'reasonableness' is particularly useful for a leaseholder as it may allow a challenge to the service charge on the basis of the quality or cost of the service provided. Section 19 of LTA 1985 now applies a statutory reasonableness test to most elements of leasehold service charges (see Chapter 4).

Implied terms

Where a service charge clause in a residential lease does not expressly import the concept of reasonableness, the courts are inclined to imply a term that the landlord is only entitled to recoup those costs that are fair and reasonable (see *Finchbourne v Rodriguez* (1976), but see also *Bandar v Darwen*, above).

Sections 13 and 15 of the Supply of Goods and Services Act 1982 require the supplier of any service to, respectively, ensure that reasonable care and skill is used and, where no amount for the service is specified, charge no more than a reasonable charge. It is not clear whether these provisions apply to leases with service charge provisions. For the most part, their significance is overtaken by the provisions of LTA 1985 (see below).

Consultation

A service charge clause may require a landlord to consult the leaseholders before embarking on a particular type of expenditure. Such provisions are not particularly common, but the lease terms should always be checked for such provision. Where a consultation provision is included, failure to comply with its strict terms may prevent a landlord recouping any costs for work subject to consultation. Consultation provisions are more likely to apply to major works than annual charges (see Chapter 5).

Method of charging

The service charge clause binds the leaseholder to pay a share of the landlord's annual costs (i.e. the total chargeable costs in any given year). This share is defined in the lease and takes one of two forms.

Fixed shares

Where there are ten nearly identical flats in a block, the lease may provide for equal shares (i.e. each leaseholder pays a one-tenth share). Alternatively, where the flats are not of equal sizes, the lease may apportion the shares equitably (i.e. leaseholders with larger flats bear a slightly larger fraction, or percentage, than the others). Fixed shares have the virtue of simplicity but, unless they contain provision for variation, do not take account of changes in the building. They may thus be susceptible to challenge on the basis that the apportionment in the light of changed circumstances is unreasonable (*Pole Properties v Feinberg* (1981)).

Variable shares

The leaseholder may be bound to pay a share calculated as the proportion that the rateable value, or floor area, of his flat bears to that of the whole building. This takes account of changes to the building and is less susceptible to challenge. Note that the abolition of domestic rating now raises difficult questions about the status of clauses that apportion service charges on the rateable value basis. Until there is a ruling from a higher court, it is unclear how effective these clauses are. Such clauses may of course be altered by agreement or by application to the court (see Chapter 8).

Difficulties in drafting can arise where particular services are enjoyed more by some leaseholders than others (e.g. some flats which consume less heat or do not require the use of a lift). Such leaseholds may divide up different elements within the service charge and apportion each element accordingly.

Drafting considerations There is a useful section on the apportionment of charges in ch.11 and annex 2 of the DoE guide of June 1995 (see Chapter 2). The annex illustrates a number of different apportionment methods. The overriding objective is that when new leases are drawn up the method of apportionment should be demonstrably fair and equitable.

Method of collection

Demands for service charge

A lease makes a leaseholder potentially liable to pay service charges and may specify a date for payment. However, until a precise charge is calculated, there is usually no liability to make a service charge payment until a demand or notification is issued to the leaseholder. The lease may specify that this is done in a particular way, for example in writing.

Interim charges

These are advance payments of service charge; the amount is determined by the wording of the lease either at the landlord's discretion or by formula (e.g. based on the previous year's annual charge). Once the landlord has arrived at a satisfactory figure for the interim charge, the landlord must usually then demand it from the leaseholder. The number and dates for payment of interim charges due are determined by the lease. There is no decided case-law in point, but it is argued that the principle in *Finchbourne v Rodriguez* (1976) (see above) applies also to interim charges.

Interim payments collected by the landlord belong, from the point of time of payment, to the landlord who is under no obligation to keep the payments separate from general funds. However, in certain circumstances, the payments are regarded as being held on trust for the lease-holders (e.g. where the lease so provides or they are set aside in a separate bank account – *see Re Chelsea Cloisters (in Liquidation)* (1980).

If the lease fails to provide for interim charges, no such provision can be implied into the lease. In these circum-stances, the service charge may be demanded as soon as the landlord is permitted to do so according to the strict wording of the service charge clause.

Annual charge

The main service charge liability is the leaseholder's share of the landlord's annual costs (i.e. the costs 'expended' or 'incurred' during the year). The relevant year (or 'accounting year') will be defined in the lease (for instance, it may commence on the same day as the commencement day of the leasehold).

Certified accounts The precise total figure of actual expendi-ture by the landlord during the year is rarely known on the last day of the relevant year. Nevertheless, the lease usually binds the landlord to provide the annual figure to the lease-holder within a certain time after the end of the year. Once the landlord has ascertained the total figure, the leaseholder is notified and the balance due demanded. The lease may require that figure be provided as detailed accounts certified, for instance, by an accountant. Such accounts may be regard-ed as a pre-condition to recovering any further service charge due (beyond that already paid as interim payments) for the year.

Providing the annual figure as soon as possible after the end of the relevant year also has obvious benefits to the leaseholder. It helps him or her raise any complaint about the whole or any part of the annual expenditure when matters are relatively recent in time. Further, in this connection, the lease may give the leaseholder rights to inspect records and invoices for the year's expenditure.

The annual expenditure figure is unlikely to be exactly the same as the total sum of interim charges collected from the leaseholder during the year. Accordingly the above procedure clarifies whether the leaseholder has paid too much or too little to the landlord; the lease should then provide for a balancing credit or charge to be made.

Where an item of the landlord's costs (e.g. maintenance cost) straddles two charging years, an apportionment is required between the two years.

Sinking funds

Where there is a 'sinking fund', interim charges and/or annual charges include a sum that is put towards the payment of service charges in a future year when they will dramatically increase due to major works. This evens out the service charge payments during the course of the leasehold and assists a leaseholder in his financial planning. Sinking funds are considered in Chapter 5.

Service charge disputes

The service charge clause may contain a provision referring any dispute about it to arbitration (note that such a provision may now be invalid under the Unfair Terms in Consumer Contracts Regulations 1994). In principle the parties to the lease are bound by this provision unless they both elect to resolve the dispute otherwise. The advantages of proceeding to arbitration, rather than to the county court, are not dealt with in this book. Note however that if a dispute is to be arbitrated, neither the parties in dispute nor the arbitration tribunal can refer the matter to a leasehold valuation tribunal under the provisions introduced in HA 1996 (see later).

Key points

- Service charges are the payments made by a leaseholder to the landlord for the cost of services, repairs, maintenance, insurance and management provided by the landlord.

- Items of a recurring nature (e.g. cleaning and caretaking) will appear each year in the service charge bill. Items such as major works of repair come round less frequently. Major works must be considered separately from annual charges.

- In any service charge matter, start with the lease. This defines what the leaseholder is bound to pay.

- The leaseholder may be charged for the costs of the performance of the landlord's covenants and/or according to a list of chargeable items and/or according to any discretionary items covered by a sweeper clause.

- If the service charge clause is defective, it may be possible to imply terms into, or vary the terms of, the lease. In particular, careful attention must be given as to whether the cost of repair and improvement work, the full cost of insurance and the cost of in-house management can be recovered.

- The lease may require, as a pre-condition to recovery, that a landlord consult leaseholders before charging for certain works or services.

- Leaseholders either pay a fixed, or variable, share of the annual service charge bill.

- Service charges are usually collected on demand by interim charges and, if the interim charges do not cover the amount actually expended, at the end of the year as a balancing charge.

- Service charge clauses may refer disputes to arbitration.

4.

Service Charges: the statutory law

Exclusions / Identifying chargeable costs /
Determination of disputes: arbitration /
Particular problems

The imposition of service charges is regulated, irrespective of a leaseholder's position under a service charge clause, by a scheme set out in sections 18-30 of the Landlord and Tenant Act (LTA) 1985. The scheme applies wherever a service charge is payable by a leaseholder of a flat (or other dwelling), as part of or in addition to rent, which varies in whole or part according to the landlord's costs (section 18). Services charges that do not vary do not fall within the scheme (see *Coventry City Council v Cole* (1993)).

Exclusions

Local authority granted leaseholds which are not 'long tenancies' are excluded (section 26(1)). A 'long tenancy' for these purposes is one which is:
1. for a term exceeding 21 years;
2. a perpetually renewable leasehold (see Chapter 1) unless it is a sub-tenancy where the immediate superior leasehold is not a long tenancy; or
3. a Part V of HA 1985 right to buy leasehold (section 26(2)).

Also excluded are section 149(6) of LPA 1925 leaseholds (see Chapter 1) unless granted by a registered housing association at a discount and complying with any relevant regulations governing shared ownership schemes (section 26(3)).

Identifying chargeable costs

A 'service charge' for the purposes of the Act specifically means a charge for 'services, repairs, maintenance, or insurance or the landlord's costs of management'. Thus the scheme applies to any variable service charge to the extent that it comprises any of these items. Given the breadth of the definition, not many items will fall outside this statutory class. But if the service charge does go further, for instance by including the cost of improvements, the LTA scheme does not regulate the additional charges, but continues to regulate those specified in the statute.

Certain particular chargeable costs require specific mention:

1. In-house management costs are included within the expression 'landlord's costs of management' (and are therefore within the scheme of regulation) because the definition of 'costs' includes 'overheads' (section 18(3)(a)).
2. Grant aided works (insofar as these are works within the statutory class); these are considered below.
3. Costs incurred by a landlord in proceedings (insofar as these are in respect of works within the statutory class) that the landlord seeks to recover through the service charge; these are considered below.

Rules regulating charging of costs

There are five rules within LTA 1985 that seek to limit the amount of costs (within the statutory class) chargeable by a landlord through the service charge.

The reasonableness rule

Irrespective of whether the lease contains an express or implied term regarding reasonableness, section 19 of LTA 1985 requires that landlord's costs (within the statutory class) may be taken into account when computing the service charge

     (a) only where they are reasonably incurred; and

     (b) where the services provided or the works carried out are of a reasonable standard.

There are few reported examples of the applications of (a) and (b) above. Any issue arising is likely to be decided on general principles of logic and fairness, taking into account all evidence before the court.

     Item (a) above prevents a landlord recouping all or part of the cost if it was unnecessary. For example, a leaseholder might regard the level of repair work undertaken (and therefore its cost) as excessive. Conflicts may also arise on duplication of costs, unreasonable delay that increased costs or exorbitant costs. Item (b) above centres more on the quality of work or services undertaken. Where the quality falls below a reasonable standard, an appropriate deduction will be made (see *Yorkbrook Investments v Batten* (1985)).

Section 19 disputes Disputes under section 19 of LTA may be resolved in the county court, the Leasehold Valuation Tribunal (LVT) or by arbitration (see below). Any term in the lease or other agreement which purports in any other way, or on specific or limited evidence, to resolve a section 19 dispute is void (section 19(3)).

The 18-month rule

Costs (within the statutory class) incurred more than 18 months before a demand is issued for them as part of the service charge cannot be recovered (section 20B(1)). This blanket rule, however, does not apply if, within 18 months beginning with the date the costs were incurred, the leaseholder is notified of them in writing and that he or she is subsequently required to pay a due proportion under the service charge (section 20B(2)).

Capital & Counties v BL plc (1987), as applied in *Westminster v Hammond* (1995), confirms the meaning of the date the costs were 'incurred' is that date when the costs fell due.

A 'demand' for the purposes of section 20B means one complying with all requirements that may be set out for demands in the service charge clause (e.g. the prior service of certified accounts). The significance of section 20B to the charging of major works through the service charge is considered in detail in Chapter 5.

Grant aided works

A grant awarded to the landlord under Part XV of HA 1985 or Part VIII of the Local Government and Housing Act 1989 towards the cost of works within the statutory charge must be deducted from the costs (and thus from the service charge) (section 20A(1)). The same applies to grants made under a Part VIII of LGHA 1989 group repair scheme for external works carried out by the landlord (section 20A(2)).

Other types of grant received do not fall within these rules and so receive no particular treatment under LTA 1985. The HA 1996 now provides for the reduction or waiving of service charges where financial assistance has been given by the Secretary of State (see Chapter 7).

Costs of proceedings

Costs (including legal costs) incurred by a landlord in proceedings (insofar as these are within the statutory class) for which recovery is sought through the service charge are covered by the section 19 reasonableness rule. Additionally, a leaseholder may apply (to the appropriate court or tribunal

– see section 20C(2)) for an order that all or any of the costs incurred before a court, the LVT or the Lands Tribunal (on appeal from the LVT) or in connection with an arbitration, are to be excluded from the service charge (section 20C(1)).

The court or tribunal may make such order as it thinks just and equitable. So, for example, where service charge provisions entitle a landlord, whether or not successful, to recover legal costs incurred, leaseholders who successfully challenge elements of their service charge and are awarded their costs (or are not required to pay the landlord's costs) can make a section 20C application to prevent the landlord recovering the legal costs through the service charge.

Major works

The limitation upon the costs chargeable where there are major works, and the LTA 1985 statutory consultation procedure (see in brief below), are considered in Chapter 5.

Consultation

Where the cost of carrying out 'works' on a block of flats or any other building exceeds the greater of £1,000 or £50 multiplied by the number of dwellings let to its leaseholders, the landlord must comply with the section 20 consultation procedure. This procedure is considered further in Chapter 5.

Accordingly, if the cost falls below the statutory levels (e.g. small day-to-day repair and maintenance) then there is no need to comply with the consultation procedure. Instead, the charge is subject only to the section 19 reasonableness rule.

The consultation rule does not apply to items under the service charge which do not involve works (e.g. insurance, caretaking charges, heating, lighting, cleaning etc.). However much these items cost, the only protection afforded to the leaseholder is in section 19.

In the main, the consultation provisions that apply to secure tenants (detailed in C. Hunter *Tenants' Rights* (Arden's

Housing Library) 1995, ch. 5) do not apply to leaseholders. Exceptions are section 27 HA 1985 (which is not often used) and section 102 HA 1988 (on which the take up has been low).

Leaseholders of properties in local authority stock which is subject to CCT, however, must be consulted about the details of contract specifications, the contractor's identity, and their entitlement to make representations to the local authority. The authority must introduce procedures whereby leaseholders can assist in monitoring the contractor's performance (see section 27A of HA 1985). This matter is dealt with in the next chapter and in C. Hunter and A. Selman, *Compulsory Competitive Tendering of Housing Management* (Arden's Housing Library) 1996, p. 33 *et seq*.

Method of charging – apportionment

The LTA 1985 does not deal specifically with the method of apportionment of service charges. Indeed any unfairness or imbalance that arises from the method of apportionment, whether between the leaseholders and the landlord or between the leaseholders themselves, is not within the ambit of section 19.

Method of collection

Interim charges

There is no restriction under LTA 1985 on the landlord requiring the payment of interim charges. The charge must, however, be reasonable. After the costs have been incurred any necessary adjustments must be made by repayment or reduction of subsequent charges (see section 19(2)). Any term in the lease or other agreement which purports to provide for the resolution of a section 19(2) dispute other than through the county court, the LVT or arbitration , or upon specific or limited evidence, is void (section 19(3)(c)).

Annual charge

The landlord is not required by any mandatory statutory rule, at the end of the service charge year, to assess the annual expenditure, or to present the annual figure to the leaseholder, in any particular way or within any particular time. Subject to the 18-month rule (see above), the parties are bound only by express requirements set out in the lease (see above).

A number of statutory provisions may be triggered, however, by the action of the leaseholder. These reflect the important policy goal that a leaseholder is entitled to information on how the annual service charge is calculated.

Section 21 of LTA 1985 Following a written request the landlord must supply the leaseholder with a written summary of the costs (within the statutory class) incurred in the previous 12 months' accounting period or, if the accounts are not made up, the previous 12 months ending with the date of the request. The landlord must provide the information within one month of the request or within six months of the end of either of the 12-month periods referred to above, whichever one is the later (section 21(1)(4)).

The written summary must:
1. identify any costs which relate to grant aided or group repair scheme works;
2. set out the costs in a way showing how they have been or will be reflected in demands for service charges; and
3. summarise any costs for which no invoice was received by the landlord within the appropriate 12-month period referred to above;
4. summarise any costs for which an invoice was received but no payment was made within the appropriate 12-month period;
5. summarise any costs for which an invoice was received and payment was made within the appropriate 12-month period;

6. specify the total service charge payment already paid by the leaseholder to the landlord to the end of the appropriate 12-month period; and
7. contain, where the service charge is payable by more than four leaseholders, a certificate by a qualified accountant that the summary is fair, supporting accounts, receipts and other documentation (see generally section 21(5) and(6)).

Having obtained the summary, the leaseholder is entitled to see the supporting documentation by written notice to the landlord within six months of receipt of the summary (section 22). The landlord must, for a period of two months, make reasonable facilities available for the inspection of the documents (for which no charge may be made), and the taking of copies (for which a reasonable charge may be made). The costs incurred by the landlord in making the facilities available may be treated as part of the management cost (section 22(6)) and recovered as such if the service charge so permits.

These rights may be exercised by the secretary of a recognised tenant's association (see Chapter 5) on the leaseholder's behalf with his or her consent (sections 21(2) and 22).

There are similar provisions where relevant costs are incurred by a superior landlord (to the leaseholder's immediate landlord) that require the immediate landlord:

1. upon a request from the leaseholder, to request a summary of the relevant costs from the superior landlord, and to pass the information received to the leaseholder; and
2. upon a request for facilities to inspect, to pass on the name and address of the superior landlord, who is then bound to provide the relevant facilities (see generally section 23).

It is a criminal offence for the landlord not to comply with these requirements (section 25). This sanction does not apply if the landlord is a local authority, a new town corporation, or the Development Board for Rural Wales (section 26) but does apply to housing associations. Local authorities have the power to prosecute any of the above offences (section 34).

Finally, the statutory requirements listed above do not appear to be satisfied by an income and expenditure account produced in accordance with standard accounting practice. Such an account fails to:

- distinguish between invoices received but not paid and invoices received and paid;
- set out the amount received from leaseholders as service charges; and
- constitute a 'summary' (i.e. a brief record).

Annual certificates Leases sometimes contain a provision that the annual certificate of expenditure shall be binding and conclusive. As stated above, any term in the lease or other agreement which purports to provide for the resolution of a section 19 dispute upon specific or limited evidence is void (section 19(3)).

Ownership of service charge monies

Sums collected by the landlord as service charge (e.g. interim payments) belong at common law to the landlord. Section 42 of LTA 1987 requires that service charges paid to a landlord, however, must now be held on trust, in a single or separate trust fund(s), to pay for the service charge and, subject to that, for the leaseholders. There are specific rules regarding the investment of the fund(s) and regarding their ownership where one or all of the relevant leaseholds have come to an end.

Local authorities and most housing associations are exempt from this provision save where their involvement in the collection of the service charge is other than in their capacity as landlord (e.g. as manager of the premises; see sections 42(1) and 58 of LTA 1987 and further below).

Sections 47 and 48 of LTA 1987

For the significance of these sections in the collection of service charges through the courts, see Chapter 9.

Determination of disputes: arbitration

Section 19 disputes

The county court has power to make a declaration in section 19 (reasonableness) disputes (section 19(4)). Additionally, HA 1996 now gives both landlords and leaseholders the right to apply to the LVT for, similarly, a determination upon any section 19 dispute (section 19(2A)). In particular, an application may be made to both the county court (see e.g. *Reston v Hudson* (1990)) and the LVT (see section 19(2B)) to establish whether the costs of proposed works will satisfy the section 19 reasonableness requirements.

Where a section 19 dispute comes before the county court which falls within the LVT's jurisdiction (i.e. where neither the leaseholder nor landlord has applied to the LVT) the court may, of its own motion, transfer the dispute to the LVT. Thereafter the county court has power, pending the LVT's determination, to deal with the outstanding proceedings as it sees fit and, upon the LVT's determination, to give effect to the determination by way of court order (section 31C).

Statutory regulations and rules of court now provide (as from 1 September 1997) for applications to, fees for, procedural rules of and transfers to the LVT. Notably the LVT has power to order from the leaseholder or landlord (or superior landlord) such information as it may reasonably require. Non-compliance is a criminal offence (section 31A(5); Schedule 22, paragraph 7 of HA 1985).

Subject to the deterrent effect of delays that may occur before LVT applications are actually heard, leaseholders are likely to make use of the LVT. No costs incurred by a party in connection with an application or transfer to the LVT are recoverable from the other side (section 31A(4) – although the fee paid may be recoverable under section 31B(2)(b). A fee of £500 is payable for proceedings before the LVT, although the LVT has power to reduce this fee according to a leaseholder's financial resources.

Section 19 disputes may be legitimately settled by arbitration. Where there is an arbitration agreement in the lease and the matter is to be referred to arbitration, no application may be made either to the county court or LVT.

Further no application may be made to the LVT where the leaseholder has agreed or admitted the amount of service charge or the matter has already been resolved in the county court or arbitration.

Other disputes

As stated above, applications under section 20C are made to the appropriate court or tribunal. Other issues under sections 20, 20A and 20B receive no particular treatment and are justiciable generally in the county court or in arbitration.

Particular problems

A number of problems, relevant to the matters raised in this chapter but not specifically addressed by the lease terms or the statutory provisions, are commonly encountered:

1. calculation of the annual service charge bill;
2. unexpected rises in the service charges; and,
3. the quality of the services provided.

Calculation of the annual service charge bill is a perennial bugbear. Landlords have to justify the figures that appear on the interim charges and other charging documents. These figures must be as accurate as possible if they are to withstand sustained scrutiny. Indeed proper calculation of the charge is a discipline all of its own. However, the fact that leaseholders may find it difficult to understand the way the calculations are done requires that effective lines of communication must exist between landlord and leaseholder. This is particularly important for social landlords.

Both landlord and leaseholder are ultimately powerless to halt rising management costs. But rises in the service charge that are not anticipated by leaseholders, as with misunderstandings regarding the calculation of service charges, are likely to lead to antagonism and dispute. So again, good communication is essential for effective leasehold management.

The quality of services provided is another source of leaseholder discontent. Effective definition of the standards required of landlords and contractors assists in creating a culture of awareness of problems (for the landlord or leaseholder) at an early stage. Procedures for monitoring the services can serve to pre-empt problems.

All these matters touch upon a general and striking theme that runs through leaseholder management, namely, that leaseholder involvement at all levels in the management of their property is a constructive course that managers are well advised to take.

Calculation of annual service charge bill

Calculation of the annual service charge bill is not in theory a difficult exercise. The service charge clause (and the legislation) is aimed at allowing the landlord to recoup costs or expenditure.

The practical problem that arises concerns the actual identification of the correct figure of total expenditure attributable to works and services carried out for the individual leaseholder's benefit. Insofar as a particular item of work or service is rendered solely for the benefit of that leaseholder, the process is simple. The full figure on the invoice is passed in its entirety to the leaseholder. However, such items are rare. Invariably, whether the leaseholder derives a benefit for work or services provided in connection with the flat, the block containing it, the surrounding estate or a wider area, the relevant work or services are part of a contract that involves providing a benefit for others also. The practical problem is then how to break down the larger invoice in such a way as to identify a fraction of the invoiced cost that may be fairly passed onto the leaseholder.

Work done which is not uniform between the respective leaseholder or tenant beneficiaries adds an extra layer of complexity to the calculation. In such circumstances equal division of the invoiced cost is inadequate. Work done under the contract over a significantly long period of time creates difficulties in identifying which leaseholders/tenants benefited in which year and splitting those benefits between charging years. The importance of good systems of preserving information about the work and the relevant documentation cannot be overstated.

The solution is to use systems of allocating and defining works contracts that link the charges to costs centres as closely as possible. A 'costs centre' is the area benefiting from the work in question, of which there are three main levels:

1. the individual flat/property (e.g. external redecoration and heating);
2. the block and its common parts (e.g. repair of the structure and common parts, building insurance, cleaning of common parts, lift repairs and maintenance, communal electricity, communal heating, supervision and management);
3. the estate and wider area (e.g. caretaking services, cleaning contracts, grounds maintenance, lighting, estate repairs).

If costs are not accurately linked to costs centres, accurate breaking down of the costs is hindered. For instance where the costs are incurred over a number of estates, the lack of precision creates difficulty for the manager attempting to split the costs between each estate. If a reasoned breakdown between the estates cannot be achieved, any attempt to split the costs equally may be susceptible to challenge (e.g. under the lease itself, on the basis that the proper cost has not been identified, or under section 19, on the basis that the amount is not reasonable).

Key points

- The important statutory provisions on service charges are sections 18-30 of the LTA 1985. The scheme applies to variable service charges that recoup the cost of services, repairs, maintenance, insurance and management provided by the landlord.
- There are five rules within the LTA 1985 scheme that limit the amount of costs chargeable by a landlord:
    1. The reasonableness rule (section 19) restricts the costs recoverable to those that are, broadly, reasonable.
    2. The major works rule (section 20) requires compliance with a statutory consultation procedure. Failure to comply limits the amounts which the landlord may recover (unless the court dispenses with the rule).
    3. The 18-month rule (section 20B(1)) prevents any costs from being recovered where the leaseholder does not receive a demand, or notification, within 18 months from the date the costs fell due.
    4. Works for which grant aid was received (section 20A(1)) cannot be charged in full to the leaseholder.
    5. The costs of legal proceedings which a landlord seeks to recover through the service charge (section 20C(1)) may be reduced or excluded entirely.
- Section 21 of LTA 1985 requires a landlord to provide a summary of, and information relating to, the costs that make up the annual charge.
- Only section 19 (and section 20C) questions can be determined, under the HA 1996, at the LVT. All other service charge disputes can be resolved in court or by arbitration.

- Calculation of the total annual service charge where the individual cost items cannot be easily allocated to individual leaseholders is difficult. The solution is to link charges to costs centres as closely as possible.
- Effective communication with leaseholders about, and involvement in, annual charging promotes good landlord and leaseholder relations and reduces the risk of service charge disputes.

5.
Service Charges: Major Works

The lease / Statutory law: LTA 1985

Major works (e.g. substantial works of repair or reconstruction, cyclical redecoration) are less frequent items of expenditure to which the leaseholder is expected to contribute. These items should be approached in precisely the same way as annual charges, namely, their recoverability is initially dependent upon the lease terms; the relevant statutory provisions then need to be considered. Accordingly, much of the previous two chapters applies to major works.

There are two fundamental reasons why major works require particular treatment. First, they are aimed at improving the building's quality, usually through repair work (in the legal sense – see Chapter 3). Yet, significantly, there may be elements of the work that go further than mere repair, which may be described as 'improvement' (see a discussion of this distinction in Chapter 3). Improvement work may not be permitted by the lease (see Chapter 8). Alternatively, even if permitted, it may not be covered by the service charge clause.

Secondly, major works are the subject of specific statutory provisions under LTA 1985.

The lease

Identifying chargeable costs

The express terms in the lease must be assessed before
commencing major works. A widely drawn service charge
clause that expressly covers improvement and repair work
means major works can be recovered through the service
charge. But a clause that covers only repair work means
the landlord must foot the bill for improvements
(see *Mullaney v Maybourne Grange (Croydon) Management
Co Ltd* (1986)). The management costs of major works
can be recovered if the clause also specifically provides
for their recovery.

Reasonableness

As with annual charges the service charge clause may
expressly state that the test of reasonableness applies to
major works costs. Alternatively, the courts may imply a
term to that effect where there is no such express term in
the lease.

Consultation

A service charge clause may expressly require a landlord to
consult leaseholders before carrying out major works. Costs
cannot be recouped if the landlord fails to perform this
obligation (see *Northways Flats Management v Wimpey Pension
Trustees* (1992)). This may apply even if statutory consultation provisions have been complied with (see below).

Method of charging

The method of charging major works is unlikely to receive
any special treatment in the lease. So leaseholders will be
charged, as for annual charges, by fixed or variable share.

The wording for apportioning the costs may be less precisely expressed than the examples given in Chapter 3. For example, a lease may state that each service charge element will be 'apportioned according to the number of units benefited by the particular item of charge' or 'reasonably apportioned'. In such a case, careful thought must be given to dividing the bill for the major works fairly.

Method of collection

Again, the service charge collection provisions are likely to apply to collecting major works costs, and interim charges levied will include an element for such costs. The final annual account will itemise the full major works costs for that year, which will form part of any certified accounts required.

Sinking Funds

Major works costs will considerably raise the service charge for the year in which they are carried out – which the leaseholder may not have budgeted for and may have difficulty paying. One way of softening the blow is to provide for a sinking fund in the lease.

Where a sinking fund is in operation, the interim and/or yearly charges include an element which is put aside in a separate fund for future major works. Over the years this separate fund builds up and pays for the major works when they become necessary. The clause covering this may be carefully worded, and may provide for such a fund for specific items such as cyclical redecoration rather than for all major works.

Calculating the 'additional' charge for the fund (over and above actual annual charges) is in theory straightforward: the landlord estimates when major works will be needed and their cost. Then the landlord collects payments from the leaseholders over time to meet that estimated cost. This is ideal for periodic items such as three – or five-yearly redecoration.

Estimation becomes more difficult for less frequently replaced items, such as a new lift. Here the landlord needs to refer to a building costs index to predict the future cost. Additionally, a surveyor's assistance will be needed to predict when the component will need replacing.

Inflation and the interest to be earned on the fund also need to be taken into account. The fund should be reviewed regularly to ensure the right target cost is met. How the fund is invested to maximum benefit and the tax position must also be considered carefully by both social and private landlords (these are outside the scope of this book and are not discussed further).

Such reasoned approach is essential to prevent the leaseholders challenging the level of charges sought (see section 19(2) of LTA 1985 discussed below).

Service charge disputes

The disputes procedure is the same as for annual charges (see Chapter 3).

Statutory law: LTA 1985

The scheme set out in sections 18-30 of LTA 1985 (see Chapter 4) applies in general to major works that fall within a service charge under section 18.

Identifying chargeable costs

The definition of 'service charge' under the 1985 Act ('services, repairs, maintenance, or insurance or the landlord's costs of management') applies to most major work elements such as redecoration and repair, but not to 'improvements'. Therefore, where a service charge clause provides that improvement costs can be recouped, the leaseholder's only challenge to the cost may be an express or implied lease term of reasonableness (see *Sutton Housing Association v Williams* (1988)).

In-house management costs for major works are included within the expression 'landlord's costs of management' (and therefore fall within the scheme of regulation) because the definition of 'costs' includes 'overheads' (section 18(3)(a)).

Rules regulating charging of costs

The LTA 1985 has five rules that seek to limit the amount of costs within the statutory class chargeable by a landlord through the service charge. In principle at least four of these are potentially applicable to the charging of major works; the rule in section 20 (consultation procedure) is of particular importance.

The reasonableness rule

Irrespective of whether a lease contains an express or implied term regarding reasonableness, section 19 of LTA 1985 requires that landlord's costs within the statutory class (therefore not including 'improvement' costs) may be taken into account when computing the service charge

    (a) only where they are reasonably incurred; and

    (b) where the services provided or the works carried out are of a reasonable standard.

In particular, section 19(2) covers situations where 'a service charge is payable before the relevant costs are incurred' and requires that:

    1. only a reasonable amount shall be payable; and

    2. after the relevant costs are incurred, any necessary adjustment is made (by repayment, reduction, subsequent charge, etc.).

This provision is apt to cover interim charges for major works and contributions to sinking funds.

The 18-month rule

This rule, discussed in detail in Chapter 4, will apply except for 'improvement' costs.

Case report

Major works took place over six months ending in February 1993. During that time interim certificates were issued under which the landlord was bound to make interim payments to the works contractors. The works contract was nevertheless a single price contract and the single price payable was only conclusively determined upon a final certificate issued in March 1994. Although general letters informing the leaseholders of their liability to pay for the works had been sent to them every six months from 1992, the first demand, for the whole sum due, was served in May 1995.

The dispute centred around whether the demand was served within 18 months of the date the costs were incurred for the purposes of section 20B(1), and whether the general letters sufficed to notify the leaseholders that the costs were to be incurred and paid for by them for the purposes of section 20B(2).

It was held that the costs were incurred at the point in time when the interim certificates were issued (at which point the contractors could have sued the landlord for the amount under the interim certificate) or (more doubtfully) at the latest when the interim payments were actually made to the landlord (all of which were made prior to April 1993). Therefore, on the facts, the May 1995 demand was out of time for the sums in all the interim certificates but not the balancing charge in the final March 1994 certificate.

The general letters did not give sufficient detail for section 20B(2) purposes. A section 20B(2) letter should state:
- that the relevant costs have been incurred;
- the nature of the works and the reason for the expenditure;

> ■ **the amount of the costs incurred and the pro-portion attributable to the individual tenant; and**
> ■ **that such amount will be demanded at some time in the future.**
> **Finally, the section 20B rule cannot be dispensed with by the court (compare section 20(9).** *Westminster v Hammond* **(1995).**

This rule can create extreme administrative difficulties for major works over a significant period of time and across a number of properties. If it is anticipated that it is not possible to bill all the leaseholders benefited by the works for the full cost of them within the 18-month period, then full notification (by means of section 20B letters) must be given to all leaseholders of the work for which interim certificates have been received.

Grant aided works

The rules for grant aided works, as discussed in Chapter 4, apply fully to major works.

Consultation

Where works costs exceed £1,000 or £50 multiplied by the number of leasehold dwellings concerned, whichever is the greater ('the statutory limit'), the landlord must comply with the section 20 statutory consultation procedure. Failure to do so prevents the landlord recovering costs which exceed the statutory limit (section 20(1)). A court has power to dispense with the consultation requirements if satisfied that the landlord has acted reasonably (section 20(9), e.g. in an emergency). Where works (on which consultation has taken place) have begun and the need for unanticipated further work is revealed, a landlord must consider carefully whether further consultation should take place or section 20(9) may be relied on.

This rule does not apply to service charge items which do not involve 'works' (e.g. insurance, caretaking charges, heating, lighting, cleaning etc.), nor to any element which constitutes 'improvement'.

There are two sets of consultation requirements: one where there is no recognised tenant's association; and the other where there is such an association. Under section 29, a recognised tenants' association means an association

1. of leaseholders (whether with or without other lease-holders or tenants) who may be required under their lease terms to contribute to the same costs by paying a service charge (section 29(1) and (4)); and

2. which is recognised as such (i.e. for LTA 1985 purposes) either in a notice in writing given by the landlord to the association's secretary (which has not been withdrawn), or in a certificate of a member of the local rent assessment committee panel (which has not been cancelled) (section 29(1)-(3)).

No recognised tenants' association Where there is no recognised tenants' association, under section 20(4), the requirements are that:

1. at least two estimates are obtained, one of them from a person wholly unconnected with the landlord;

2. a notice accompanied by a copy of the estimates is given to each leaseholder concerned or displayed where it is likely to come to the leaseholders' notice;

3. the notice describes the works to be carried out and invites observations on them and on the estimates, and states the name and UK address of the person to whom the observations may be sent and the date by which they must be received;

4. the above date is not earlier than one month after the date on which the notice is given or displayed;

5. the landlord has regard to any observations received and, unless they are urgently required, the works are not begun earlier than the date specified in the notice.

Existing recognised tenants' association Where there is a recognised tenants' association, under section 20(5) and (6) the requirements are that:

1. the landlord gives to the association's secretary a notice containing a detailed specification of the works in question and specifying a reasonable period within which the association may propose the names of one or more persons from whom estimates for the works should in its view be obtained by the landlord;

2. at least two estimates are obtained, one of them from a person wholly unconnected with the landlord;

3. a copy of each estimate is given to the association's secretary;

4. a notice is given to each leaseholder concerned represented by the association which

- describes briefly the works to be carried out;
- summarises the estimates (unless copies of the estimates are enclosed with the notice);
- informs the leaseholder that he or she has a right to inspect and take copies of a detailed specification of the works and of the estimates (unless copies of the estimates are enclosed with the notice);
- invite observations on these works and estimates; and
- specify the name and UK address of the person to whom the observations may be sent and the date by which they must be received;

5. the date stated in the notice is not earlier than one month after the date on which the notice is given;

6. if any leaseholder to whom a notice is given so requests, the landlord shall afford that person reasonable facilities to inspect a detailed specification of the works and the estimates, free of charge, and for taking

copies for a reasonable charge set by the landlord (unless copies of the estimates were enclosed with the notice); and

7. the landlord has regard to any observations received in pursuance of the notice and, unless they are urgently required, the works are not begun earlier than the date specified in the notice.

Any costs incurred for providing facilities for inspection or copying may be recovered as management costs through the service charge clause (section 20(7)).

Under section 20(5) notice must be given (e.g. by post) to each leaseholder. Many landlords follow this practice where section 20(4) applies (rather than by using a notice board). A landlord must then consider any responses received from the leaseholders and must take account of any reasonable objections, say, on the question of costs. Failure to do so will constitute non-compliance with section 20.

These provisions reflect what many landlords would regard as good practice. Consultation with leaseholders always tends to minimise disputes: leaseholders are made aware of the likely cost at the earliest point in time and contribute to the decision-making process.

Other rights of a recognised tenants' association
- To appoint a surveyor to advise on service charges (section 84 of HA 1996).
- To obtain a written summary of insurance cover (section 30A of LTA 1985).
- To obtain details of any managing agents (section 30B of LTA 1985) – see generally Chapter 8.

Section 20 and compulsory competitive tendering The competitive tendering regime creates potential difficulty for local authorities. Although some CCT contracts only require the contractor to do minor responsive repairs, other contractors are awarded 'term contracts' to repair and maintain housing stock for several years, as and when the landlord requires them to. This effectively undermines the section 20 consultation rights for two estimates to be raised.

There are no easy solutions to this. One way is for the landlord to restrict term contracts to jobs which fall below the statutory limit costs. Another is to introduce the consultation procedure during the negotiation stage, before the contract is awarded.

It might even be argued that by invoking section 20(9) in the light of:

1. the costs benefits to leaseholders under term contracts,
2. the administrative difficulties in carrying out the consultation procedure (and any consequent rise in the in-house management costs), and
3. the fact that some consultation has taken place under CCT requirements,

the landlord has acted reasonably and that the consultation procedure can be dispensed with. This argument may be worth pursuing where the problem has already arisen. It should not be relied on if either of the above alternatives is still available. There is an obvious need for the legislative statutory limit provisions to be reviewed.

Method of charging

As for annual charges, the LTA 1985 does not deal specifically with the method of apportionment of service charges. Any unfairness or imbalance that arises from such method is not within the ambit of section 19.

Method of collection

Sections 47 and 48 of LTA 1987 and sections 19(3), 21-23 and 25 of LTA 1985 apply to service charges that include sums attributable to major works in the same way as for annual charges (see Chapter 4).

Section 42 of LTA 1987 does not apply to local authorities and most housing associations. Nonetheless, it is good practice to maintain sinking funds in separate accounts.

Determination of disputes: arbitration

Determination of disputes involving major works charges, whether they are section 19, 20, 20A, 20B or 20C disputes, are dealt with in the same way as those involving only annual charges (see Chapter 4).

Key points

- Major works may involve 'improvement' work. The lease should be checked to see if the cost of such work is recoverable.
- Express consultation requirements in the lease should be complied with before major works are undertaken.
- Sinking funds for major works should be used where provided for in the lease terms.
- The LTA 1985 regulates the charging of major works (but not 'improvement' work) in the same way as annual charges:
  - (a) The section 19 reasonableness test applies to major works and, in particular, to the level of contributions made by a leaseholder to a sinking fund.
  - (b) The charging of long term major works projects must comply with section 20B. Consideration should always be given to serving section 20B(2) letters.
  - (c) The section 20 consultation procedure must always be complied with, except in an emergency.

6.
Service Charges and Improvement Contributions: right to buy and acquire leases

Housing Act 1980 / Housing and Building
Control Act 1984 / Housing Act 1985 /
Housing and Planning Act 1987 /
Leasehold Reform, Housing and Urban
Development Act 1993 / Housing Act 1996

A right to buy lease, like any other, must be read according to its strict wording. The discussion in Chapter 3 therefore applies to these leases. The LTA 1985 provisions discussed in Chapters 4 and 5 also apply.

Nevertheless, right to buy leases merit particular consideration because of provisions which:

- render the leaseholder liable for the cost of making good 'structural defects' in certain circumstances
- limit the amount of service charge (and other sums) recoverable from the leaseholder
- render the leaseholder liable for 'improvement contributions'.

These provisions have changed somewhat since right to buy was first introduced in 1980. Accordingly, the terms of leases granted prior to 1987 are different to those granted since then under the present provisions.

Non-right to buy leaseholders are rarely obliged to pay open-ended contributions towards improvements made to their block. Given that most right to buy leaseholders are former secure tenants on low incomes, heavy financial charges can become a burden to them; in fact, many have been given bills for works that they cannot pay. Sections 219 and 220 of HA 1996 (discussed in Chapter 7) specifically seek to address this problem.

Housing Act 1980

This Act gave secure tenants the right to buy. Under the new scheme a landlord was obliged to keep the dwelling's structure and exterior, and the building containing it, in repair and to make good any structural defect (Schedule 2, paragraph 13). A landlord could require a leaseholder to bear a reasonable part of the costs of

1. carrying out repairs, and/or
2. making good structural defects if
   (a) the leaseholder was notified of them before entering into the lease, or
   (b) the landlord was not aware of any defect until 10 years after the date the lease was granted (Schedule 2, paragraph 16).

The leaseholder could also be required to pay a reasonable part of the landlord's insurance costs. If the landlord wished to include such terms in the lease, such terms were proposed in preliminary notice served by the landlord on the secure tenant. This notice was known as 'the section 10' notice.

Accordingly a landlord could stipulate that not only was a leaseholder responsible under the service charge for the costs of repairs but also for making good structural defects. The latter liability would be operative from the start of the leasehold (if notification of the defects was given) or after ten years (where there was no notification and/or the landlord did not become aware of defects within the first ten years).

Structural defects

The Act does not define 'structural defects'; neither is there any case-law which considers a definition. The expression means defects to the 'structure'. The 'structure' of a building is confined to the particular parts which are essential to the building's physical integrity.

The liability to pay towards the cost of making good defects under these provisions is open ended and potentially high. Further, it may not be clear how putting right a structural defect is to be paid for (i.e. under the landlord's ordinary obligation to repair – and recoup costs through the service charge, or the landlord's separate obligation to make good a defect – and recoup costs as additional payments from the leaseholder). See further A. Kilpatrick, *Repairs and Maintenance* (Arden's Housing Library) 1996, Ch. 2.

Housing and Building Control Act 1984

Section 7(3) of this Act amended the rule in Schedule 2, paragraph 16 of HA 1980 in the leaseholder's favour. After 1984, a landlord could require a leaseholder to bear a reasonable part of the costs of making good any structural defect if
1. the landlord notified the leaseholder, in the preliminary section 10 notice, of both the defect and an estimated amount of how much the leaseholder was expected to pay towards making it good, or
2. the landlord did not become aware of the defect until 10 years after the date the lease was granted.

The HBCA 1984 went further by introducing a more comprehensive preliminary section 10 notice. The landlord became responsible not only for setting out the proposed terms of the leasehold grant but, if those included a provision enabling the landlord to recover service charges from the leaseholder, the notice had to state the estimated average annual amount payable for each element of the service charge and the total of those estimated amounts. Thereafter the section 10 notice made right to buy leaseholders more aware of their foreseeable liabilities under the service charge clause.

Housing Act 1985

This statute consolidated the provisions of the HA 1980 and HBCA 1984. The preliminary notice is now known as 'the section 125' notice.

Housing and Planning Act 1986

This Act amended the service charge and improvement contribution provisions for right to buy leaseholders as from 7 January 1987. The amendments regulate all new leases granted under right to buy.

Landlords' and leaseholders' obligations: present position

First, as seen in Chapter 2 and consistent with the original 1980 provisions, a landlord remains obliged to carry out repairs and make good structural defects and reinstate the block, or flat, if damaged or destroyed in circumstance that are normally covered by insurance (paragraphs 14(2), (3), Schedule 6 of HA 1985).

Secondly, the leaseholder may have to bear a reasonable part of the repair and making good costs (as 'service charges') and insurance costs (paragraph 16A, Schedule 6, HA 1985 and see Chapter 2). In respect of other service charge items, there is only a requirement that a clause permitting their recovery is reasonable in all the circumstances (paragraph 5, Schedule 6, HA 1985).

Thirdly, (impliedly) the leaseholder may have to pay 'improvement contributions' for improvements to the flat, the block containing it or any other building (i.e. one that the leaseholder has the benefit of under the lease, e.g. a garage (section 187 of HA 1985)). 'Improvement' for these purposes may go further than mere repair or making good structural defects (see A. Kilpatrick, *Repairs and Maintenance* (Arden's Housing Library) 1996, Ch. 2). Again, the only requirement is that a covenant requiring the leaseholder to pay improvement contributions is reasonable in all the circumstances (paragraph 5, Schedule 6 of HA 1985).

Restrictions on charging: present position

If the leaseholder is required to pay service charges, the section 125 notice must contain the following:
1. The landlord's estimate of the average annual amount (at current prices) payable under each head of the service charge during the 'reference period' (section 125A of HA 1985). The reference period starts with a specified date, within six months after the section 125 notice is given, by which date the landlord reasonably considers the lease will have been granted. It ends:
   (a) exactly five years after the specified date; or
   (b) where the section 125 notice proposes that service charges will be payable in connection with a specified annual period at the end of the fifth such annual period beginning after the starting date (section 125C HA 1985)
2. details of any structural defects known to the landlord (section 125 of HA 1985)
3. for purchasers of flats, the service charge element relating to prospective repairs (including making good of structural defects) set out separately with estimates for

specific works which the landlord considers may be incurred during the reference period and for the average annual amount of general repair work envisaged (section 125A of HA 1985).

Similarly, if the leaseholder is required to pay improvement contributions, the notice must set out a list of the improvements which the landlord considers may be needed during the reference period, and their estimated costs (section 125B of HA 1985).

The notice must also inform the purchaser that the landlord is limited to recovering service charges in respect of repairs (including but not limited to the cost of the landlord performing obligations under paragraph 14(2), Schedule 6 – see above) and improvement contributions at the estimated sums given (sections 125A and 125B(1) of HA 1985). An allowance can be made for inflation (Housing (Right to Buy) (Service Charges) Order 1986 (SI No 2195)). These limitations are prescribed by Schedule 6, paragraphs 16B and 16C to HA 1985 and apply during the 'initial period' of the lease. The section 125 notice must also inform the purchaser of a right to a loan to pay service charges (see Chapter 7).

The initial period

The 'initial period' of the lease is defined as a five year period from the grant of the lease, except where:
1. the service charges or improvement contributions are to include costs incurred in a period before the grant of the lease, in which case the initial period begins with the beginning of that period; or
2. the lease provides for service charges or improvement contributions to be calculated by reference to a specific annual period, the initial period continues until the end of the fifth such period beginning after the grant of the lease.

The 'initial period' and the section 125 notice 'reference period' may therefore not be concurrent (see the example below).

Where estimated costs of works of repair and improvement contributions are provided in the notice, the leaseholder does not have to pay more in the initial period than the estimated amount (irrespective of whether the initial period and reference period are concurrent). For repairs which are not itemised in the notice, the leaseholder does not have to pay more than:

1. as regards parts of the initial period falling within the reference period, the estimated annual average amount given in the notice; and
2. as regards parts of the initial period not falling within the reference period, the average rate produced by averaging over the reference period all works for which estimates are contained in the notice.

Examples

(a) A section 125 notice is served on a secure tenant on 1 January 1997. The landlord anticipates that completion can be effected by 1 April 1997 and specifies this date as the reference period start date (i.e. within six months of 1 January). The notice does not provide for service charges or improvement contributions to be calculated by reference to a specific annual period. The reference period therefore ends on 31 March 2002 (i.e. five years from the start date). The notice gives estimates for the reference period of: £250 for itemised repairs; £100 each year for non-itemised repairs; and, zero for improvement contributions.

Subsequently the grant is delayed and takes place on 1 July 1997 (which is the start date for the initial period). The initial period therefore ends on 30 June 2002.

Between 1 July 1997 and 31 March 2002 the landlord may charge in accordance with the notice (i.e. £250 for itemised works and at the rate of £100 each year for non-itemised works). Between 31 March 2002 and 30 June 2002, the repairs charge may not exceed the rate of £50 each year (that is, the average created by dividing the itemised work cost of £250 by 5 (the reference period)). For those three months the charge would be £16.66.

(b) Suppose the above notice had stated that service charges and improvement contributions were to be calculated in connection with costs incurred between 1 January and 31 December of any given year. The reference period start date would be 1 April 1997 but the period would end on 30 December 2003 (i.e. the end of the fifth period of 1 January to 30 December beginning after 1 April 1997). The initial period would run from 1 July 1997 to 30 December 2003.

(c) Suppose, in situation (b), the section 125 notice also proposes to make the leaseholder liable for service charges in respect of costs incurred from 1 January 1997 (see further, J Henderson, *Rights to Buy and Acquire* (Arden's Housing Library) 1997). The reference period would be as in (b), but the initial period would run from 1 January 1997 to 31 December 2002 (i.e. there would be a period where the initial period did not fall within the reference period prior to the reference period starting).

Although the section 125 notice must set out an estimate of the average annual amount of other elements of the service charge (i.e. non-repair work), the estimates in the notice for this work do not constitute a limit upon the level of charge for non-repair items in the initial period. A leaseholder from whom charges in excess of the estimates are sought may however have a claim in misrepresentation (*Heinemann v Cooper* (1987)).

Leasehold Reform, Housing and Urban Development Act 1993

Under LRHUDA 1993 the service charge/improvement contributions payable by a rent to mortgage leaseholder are reduced in proportion to the landlord's share of the property; this must be expressed as percentages (Schedule 6, paragraph 16E to HA 1985). This operates as a general principle. Rent to mortgage leaseholders are entitled to the statutory limitation upon service charges during the initial period.

Housing Act 1996

Right to acquire leaseholds are subject to the same terms as ordinary right to buy leaseholds (see the Housing (Right to Acquire) Regulations 1997). Accordingly, what is said above applies equally to right to acquire leaseholds.

Key points

- Under early right to buy leases, the rights and duties of the landlord and leaseholder are different to today's. In particular, a leaseholder may be liable for the landlord's costs of making good structural defects if the leaseholder has been notified of the defects (and, after 1984, of the costs) or the landlord does not find out about the defects until after 10 years from the grant date.
- After the HPA 1986 the rules are as follows:
  - (a) Leaseholders are usually bound to pay service charges and improvement contributions. The express terms of their leases must be read to identify which charges they may be liable for (see Chapter 3).
  - (b) Leaseholders can only be charged:
    - a reasonable part of the repair cost for the flat/block's structure and exterior (including the making good of structural defects);
    - a reasonable part of the insurance cost; and
    - for all repair work and improvements, up to (but not in excess of) the estimate figures provided in the section 125 notice.

   (c) Leaseholders can be charged for all non-repair items of service charge in excess of the estimate figures provided in the section 25 notice (but a claim for misrepresentation may be available).

- All right to buy and acquire leaseholders have the benefit of sections 18-30 of LTA 1985 (see Chapters 4 and 5).

7.
Recovery of Service Charges

Inability to pay / Resolving disputes and enforcing payment

A leaseholder may not want to pay a service charge for two possible reasons:

1. he or she disputes all or part of the amount demanded; and/or
2. he or she cannot afford to pay it because
   (a) he or she has a low income;
   (b) the maintenance costs are high; or
   (c) the bill is for major works.

For 1. and 2.(c) above, the landlord must fully justify the amount demanded.

This chapter covers two topics: the assistance available to leaseholders unable to pay; and the steps a landlord can take to enforce payment.

Inability to pay

Leaseholders with high service charges may be assisted in a number of ways and it is good practice for social landlords to advise leaseholders of the assistance available. Sinking funds, as discussed in Chapter 5, can ease the burden of major works costs.

Housing (Service Charge Loans) Regulations 1992

Right to buy leaseholders have the right to a loan to help with service charges for repairs (including those to structural defects) that are payable in the first ten years of the lease. This does not however apply to improvements.

The 1992 Regulations (which do not apply to leaseholders under the preserved right to buy), made under section 450A of HA 1985, provide that the right to a loan arises only where repair costs:

1. exceed £1,500 (less any service charge amount already demanded); and
2. do not exceed £20,000 (less any outstanding loan amount under the 1992 Regulations).

The minimum loan is £501. (All the aforementioned figures are adjusted annually by reference to the retail price index).

Where the landlord is a local authority, the right to a loan entitles the local authority to leave the whole or part of the service charge due outstanding. Where the landlord is a housing association, the right is to an advance from the Housing Corporation or Housing for Wales. In both cases the loan is secured against the leasehold (see section 450A(4) and (7) of HA 1985).

The Regulations set out the loan procedure. They impose a duty on landlords to inform leaseholders of their entitlement to a loan towards repair costs (regulation 4). The loan terms are set out in regulation 6 and Schedules 1 and 2 to the Regulations. These deal with repayment and the relevant rate of interest charged. However, the interest rates are high and have made such loans unpopular.

These loan provisions do not apply to leaseholders under the new right to acquire.

Section 450B of the 1985 Act provides that loans may be made towards repair costs to leaseholders holding long leases where section 450A does not apply. The loan procedure is the same as above.

Income support and housing benefit

Leaseholders can claim income support for housing costs. Two conditions must be satisfied to qualify:

1. the claimant must be the person paying those costs; and
2. that claimant must occupy the premises being claimed as his or her home.

Claims can be made for interest payments on loans for some repairs and improvements; ground rent for long leaseholders; and some service charges (e.g. caretaking, some repairs and improvements costs, garden maintenance, lift maintenance, insurance premiums for common insurance policies). They cannot be made for the costs of heating, water and electricity charges (see further Income Support (General) Regulations 1987, Schedule 3, as amended).

Some shared ownership scheme leaseholders may be entitled to housing benefit for the rental element of their costs.

Renovation and common parts grants

The Housing Grants, Construction and Renovation Act 1996 introduced a new scheme for local authorities to award grants to improve and repair dwellings. A grant for a flat is a 'renovation grant'; a grant for common parts of a building is a 'common parts grant'.

Full details are beyond the scope of this book, but note the following outline points:

1. Unless good reasons are given or statutory exceptions apply, grants cannot be approved where work has already begun (section 29). Thus a leaseholder must be informed that grants are available and of when the works will commence to apply for a grant in good time.
2. For renovation grants, applicants must have had a three-year interest in the flat and intend to continue living there for at least another five years once the work is finished (sections 8 and 11).

3. For common parts grants, at least 75 per cent of the flats must be occupied by 'occupying tenants'. Further, at least 75 per cent of those tenants must have a duty to carry out or contribute to the work (sections 14 and 15).

4. The amount awarded is calculated by means testing (sections 30 and 32).

Hardship schemes

Some social landlords have established hardship schemes which offer loans at low or no interest, deferred repayment and writing off the debt entirely.

For local authorities, the question has arisen whether officers implementing such schemes are in breach of their fiduciary duties to collect the full service charge amount owed. Indeed questions over the legitimacy of such schemes resulted in the introduction of DoE guidance (June 1995 – which should be treated with caution) and now sections 219 and 220 of HA 1996 (see below). Housing associations on the other hand, to some of which the section 219 and 220 provisions also apply, have developed a variety of individual schemes.

The practice of delayed billing to assist leaseholders with costs runs the risk of rendering the entire service charge costs unrecoverable (see section 20B LTA of 1985 above).

Social Landlords Mandatory and Discretionary Reduction of Service Charges (England) Directions 1997

The Secretary of State may issue directions requiring or permitting social landlords to waive or reduce service charges (sections 219 and 220 of HA 1996). Under this power, the Social Landlords Mandatory Reduction of Service Charges (England) Directions 1997 ('the Mandatory Directions') and the Social Landlords Discretionary Reduction of Service Charges (England) Directions 1997 ('the Discretionary Directions') have been introduced with effect from 25

February 1997. These Directions apply to service charges in respect of repair, maintenance and improvement.

These Directions cover two distinct situations. First, they address circumstances where social landlords have received specific additional funding for works carried out on their stock (e.g. Estate Action Schemes). Where these works benefited leaseholders bound by their service charge clauses to contribute to their costs, landlords found themselves recouping sums already covered (at least in part) by the funding (compare the operation of section 20A of LTA 1985 in Chapter 4).

Secondly, more generally, the Discretionary Directions address the general problem of high service charges raised against poorer leaseholders (e.g. right to buy leaseholders).

Mandatory Directions

The Mandatory Directions apply to social landlords recovering costs from leaseholders for works wholly or partly funded through the Single Regeneration Budget Challenge Fund or the Estates Renewal Challenge Fund ('the Funds'), where the application for funds is made on or after 25 February 1997.

Paragraph 3.1 Subject to paragraphs 3.2 and 4 (see below), a landlord cannot charge for works costs (whether wholly or partly funded on one or more occasions) which exceed a total of £10,000 for the same leasehold property in any five-year period.

> **Example**
>
> Works are carried out on X's flat in 1997-98 and 1998-99 as part of an ERCF scheme. These cost £7,000 (£3,500 being chargeable in each year). Between 1999 and 2002 the landlord effects further works, with ERCF assistance, worth £10,000. As the total charge during the period 1997-98 to 2001-02 totals £17,000, the landlord must reduce charges in the later years by £7,000.

Paragraph 3.2 If a landlord considers works have benefited a leasehold property by over £10,000 over that five-year period, and also has:

1. sent a written calculation of the estimated benefit to the leaseholder,
2. allowed the leaseholder from receipt of the calculation at least 28 days to make representations on it,
3. considered any representations made, and
4. sent the leaseholder the decision made on those representations,

then subject to Paragraph 4 (below), the landlord is not obliged to reduce the charge to £10,000. But the landlord cannot charge in excess of the calculated benefit. Here, 'benefit' means an increase in the leasehold value (including any reduction of negative value) resulting from repairs, maintenance or improvements.

> **Example**
>
> In the above example, if **X**'s property over the above period increased from £40,000 to £52,000 in value as a result of the works, the landlord is not bound to limit the charge to £10,000 over the relevant period but may charge £12,000.

Paragraph 4 A landlord may propose in an application for assistance funds to reduce the service charges in any five-year period to below £10,000. Once the application and service charges are approved by the Secretary of State, the landlord cannot seek to recover higher than specified service charges. The Secretary of State may alter the maximum service charge applied for in agreement with the landlord.

> **Example**
>
> ERCF assistance is applied for in 1997-98. It is estimated that the works affecting leaseholders' flats over a five-year period will cost £17,000 each. However the flats are likely to increase in value

only by £6,000 each as a result of the works. In the application for assistance the landlord specifies £6,000 as the maximum service charge to be made of each leaseholder and, once agreed, is thereby bound to charge no more than that. Of course, the landlord is not bound to restrict the charge to £6,000 in the application and could stipulate a figure up to £10,000.

Discretionary Directions

The Discretionary Directions apply to social landlords making a service charge which is payable by a leaseholder.

Grant funded schemes Paragraph 4 applies to landlords recovering costs from leaseholders for works wholly or partly funded through Estate Action, City Challenge, the Single Regeneration Budget Challenge Fund or the Estates Renewal Challenge Fund, where the application for funds is made before 25 February 1997. The landlord, under paragraph 6, may waive or reduce the charge provided the total waiver or reduction does not exceed the total funds received to assist costs attributable to the leasehold properties.

Criteria When considering waivers and reductions, the landlord must look at each leaseholder's individual circumstance, as follows:
1. Was the leaseholder, before purchasing the leasehold, made aware of the estimated works costs (e.g. by a section 125 notice – see Chapter 6)?
2. Did the purchase price take account of these costs?
3. Has the leaseholder benefited, or will he or she benefit, from the works (e.g. increased leasehold value, reduction in negative equity, increased energy efficiency, improved security (such as increased safety from fire, theft or accident), improved services or facilities?

4. Will the leaseholder suffer exceptional hardship (see below)?
5. Are there other circumstances the landlord considers relevant?

Exceptional hardship Paragraph 7 sets out the criteria upon which a leaseholder's application on grounds of exceptional hardship must be judged. These are:
1. whether the flat is the leaseholder's only or principal home;
2. the total amount of service charges paid or payable since the flat was purchased;
3. the amount of the service charge payable in the year the exceptional hardship application is made;
4. the financial resources available to the leaseholder (here DoE guidance, February 1997, suggests that local authorities may wish to apply the means test applied in the house renovation and disabled facilities grants regime);
5. whether the leaseholder can take out a mortgage or bank loan or has other means of raising the funds;
6. whether the leaseholder can pay the charge over an extended period; and
7. any other circumstance the landlord considers relevant (e.g. age or infirmity).

Example

A local authority receives £2 million through assistance funds to refurbish blocks of flats. The element benefiting the leaseholder units is calculated at £100,000. First, over the relevant service charge years, the maximum amount of service charge reduction that may be given collectively between all the leaseholders is £100,000 (i.e. a complete waiver). Secondly, waiver or reductions of individual service charge bills must be effected according to paragraph 6 criteria. Some leaseholders' charges may be waived in their entirety because they received no benefit from the works

> or, after application, have been found to be in exceptional hardship. Others may have their bills reduced, in accordance with the paragraph 6 criteria, in line with the decreasing benefit they have derived from the work.

General discretion to reduce charges Under paragraph 5, where service charges (whether paid or payable) exceed £10,000 for the same leasehold property in any five-year period, a landlord may waive or reduce charges for poorer leaseholders with high service charges. They must not be waived or reduced to less than £10,000 for the same property in the same five-year period. The paragraph 6 and 7 criterion apply.

> **Example**
>
> **Works carried out to Z's flat between 1992-93 and 1996-97 cost £17,000. Over the five-year period this exceeds the £10,000 benchmark by £7,000. Depending on the criteria relevant in Z's case, the local authority may**
> > **(a) reduce the bill by the full £7,000 (where Z has a compelling case on grounds of poverty);**
> > **(b) reduce the bill by less than £7,000; or**
> > **(c) make no reduction at all.**

Some concern has been expressed at the way local authorities should exercise their discretion under these Directions. By using the discretion, an authority foregoes income which has to be made up from its own resources. DoE guidance (February 1997, paragraph 22) provides little assistance and states:

> '[A local authority's] discretion to reduce service charges does not over-ride any legislation or other rules under which [local authorities] operate. In particular [they] will need to balance this new discretion against [their] general fiduciary duty to local

> tax payers or others, including [their] tenants. But if
> [they] follow the criteria [i.e. in paragraph 6 of the
> Directions], and have a record to show how [they]
> have done so in a given case, this should help [them]
> to demonstrate to [their] auditors and others how
> [they] have complied with their general obligations.'

It remains to be seen how individual authorities will approach these provisions.

Mortgagees

Leaseholders' mortgagees (e.g. building societies) are a possible source of finance for service charge bills that cannot be paid. A second charge for the unpaid amount may be taken over the property. Alternatively, the mortgage repayments may be re-scheduled in such a way as to make the service charge payable.

Mortgagee protection – shared ownership

As discussed in Chapter 2, shared ownership leases often contain mortgagee protection clauses. The implications of these for landlords where the leaseholder is in financial trouble are that the mortgagee may choose to surrender the leasehold to the landlord thereby obliging the landlord to pay off the arrears (as defined by formula in the lease provisions).

Alternatively, any attempt to forfeit the leasehold for non-payment of sums due results in the mortgagee seeking relief from forfeiture (see Chapter 9) and thereafter selling the leasehold. Although the full debt (plus costs etc.) owed to the mortgagee is likely to be repaid by this course of events, this may not necessarily result in the landlord recovering the full amount due for the remaining equity.

Resolving disputes and enforcing payment

Section 94 of HA 1996

The Secretary of State may give financial assistance to any person providing general legal advice about any aspect of

- landlord and tenant so far as it relates to residential leasehold, or
- estate management schemes in connection with enfranchisement (under LRHUDA 1993 see below Chapter 12).

Internal procedures

Service charge disputes may be resolved firsthand by social landlords within internal mechanisms (such as internal arbitration). For housing associations, there is guidance on creating such mechanisms in 'The Leaseholder's Guarantee' (see para. F7) and the 'ARHM Code' (see para. 12).

Ombudsman services

Local authority leaseholders may complain to their housing department, their councillor or take up matters of maladministration with the Local Authority Ombudsman. Housing association leaseholders were able to take up matters of maladministration with the Housing Association Tenants' Service Ombudsman. Now section 51 and Schedule 2 to HA 1996 provides for a new statutory Ombudsman scheme which all social landlords must join.

Legal proceedings

If legal proceedings are contemplated against a leaseholder there are two routes to enforcement: an action for arrears of service charge, which if successful would be followed by enforcement of the judgement; or the landlord may seek forfeiture (termination) of the leasehold to force indirectly the leaseholder to pay the sums owed (see Chapter 9). It is uncommon for social landlords to take the forfeiture route; it is now only possible to do so where the amount of service charge owing has been clearly quantified.

A dispute over arrears may, under the lease terms, be the subject of an enforceable arbitration clause (see Chapter 3), in which case the landlord may be prevented from suing in the county court. Alternatively, even where a landlord legitimately commences county court proceedings, the matter may be referred to the Leasehold Valuation Tribunal (see Chapter 4).

Self Help

If a leaseholder fails to pay rent, a landlord is entitled to the self help remedy of 'distress'. The landlord is entitled to seize and sell goods at the property belonging to the leaseholder to satisfy the arrears. If service charges or sums due for insurance are reserved as if they were rent (see Chapter 9), distress may be sought for arrears of those.

The procedure for carrying out distress is technical and carries penalties for landlords who break the rules. Careful consideration should be given before using this method of recovery.

Key points

- Assistance to leaseholders unable to pay service charges may take the form of:
  1. a service charge loan, available during the first ten years of the leasehold but at unattractive interest rates;
  2. income support or housing benefit;
  3. renovation and common parts grants, usually applied for before works are begun and means tested;
  4. mandatory reduction of the charge, available in con-nection with grant funded schemes and, unless speci-

fically overridden, confining works charges to £10,000 over five years;

5. discretionary reduction of the charge, available in connection with grant funded schemes (where, in accordance with set criteria, the charge may be offset in whole or part by the funding) or if service charges exceed £10,000 over five years (where, in accordance with the criteria, the charges may be reduced to £10,000 for the same period);

6. further financing from a mortgagee.

  ▪ A leaseholder may apply under section 96 of HA 1996 for financial assistance to obtain legal advice in connection with a residential leasehold matter.

  ▪ Enforcement proceedings may take the form of an arrears action or a forfeiture action (see Chapter 9). Service charge disputes may now be referred to the Leasehold Valuation Tribunal (see Chapter 4).

Part III

8.
Covenants and Regulation of Management

The covenants / Variation of covenants /
Regulation of management

This chapter discusses three matters related to but distinct from service charges: the remaining covenants in the lease; variation of covenants; and regulation of leasehold management.

The covenants

Repairs

Commonly, the landlord is responsible for all important repairs (e.g. the block's structure and exterior; rainwater ducts, pipes, drains, electrics and installations; the common parts within the block; and communal areas beyond the block). This is in part because enforcing repairing covenants against a leaseholder can be difficult. Where such responsibility falls on the leaseholder, there may be a covenant to allow the landlord to enter and effect repair after the leaseholder defaults and to recover the costs from the leaseholder.

Both landlord and leaseholder should be aware of their level of responsibility (e.g. for either repair or renewal and replacement). Covenants for commonly disputed matters, such as whether doors and windows are part of the main walls or structure should be clearly worded. If a clause is inadequately worded and no term as to repair can be implied or agreed, a variation can be applied for (see below). Section 20 of LTA 1985 should be complied with before major works are carried out (see Chapter 5).

Enforcement of the repairing covenant against a landlord is considered in detail in A. Kilpatrick, *Repairs and Maintenance* (Arden's Housing Library) 1995, Ch. 5. Many of the remedies discussed there are available to leaseholders (i.e. specific performance and damages). For the landlord's remedies, see further Chapter 9 below.

Alterations and improvements

Normally, leases absolutely prohibit the leaseholder from making alterations to the structure or load bearing walls of the block.

They may also absolutely prohibit any alterations to non-load bearing walls or other parts of the flat, or permit such alterations only with the landlord's prior consent. A covenant may expressly stipulate that a landlord cannot unreasonably withhold consent. If it does not, section 19(2) of LTA 1927 provides similarly, notwithstanding any provision to the contrary, that the landlord cannot unreasonably withhold consent to any alteration that is an improvement.

An improvement for these purposes is judged from the leaseholder's point of view (see *Woolworth v Lambert* (1937)).

Under section 19(2), as a requirement of providing consent, a landlord may require:

1. compensation for damage done by the 'improvement';
2. reimbursement of costs incurred in giving consent; and
3. where the improvement does not add to the letting

value, an undertaking from the leaseholder that the flat will be re-instated to its former condition.

A serious breach of this covenant by a leaseholder is likely to result in forfeiture proceedings (see further Chapter 9).

Social landlords may reserve the right to improve a block of flats (and seek contributions from leaseholders – see Chapter 6). If the landlord is likely to require access to the leaseholder's flat in order properly to carry out works of alteration or improvement to the block (e.g. common parts), then an express right of access should be reserved in the lease. If no such right is reserved, and the leaseholder refuses access, the landlord can apply for an access order under section 1 of the Access to Neighbouring Land Act 1992. The court will make the order only if it is satisfied that such access is reasonably necessary (section 1(2),(3)). Access orders can facilitate the making of improvements to the block (section 1(4),(5)).

By contrast, if the landlord requires access to the flat to carry out works of alteration or improvement to any part of the flat demised to the leaseholder, the landlord must expressly reserve the right to enter and effect the works in the lease. In the absence of such an express term or agreement between the parties, the landlord is not entitled to interfere with the leaseholder's holding. An application by the landlord to vary the lease under LTA 1987 would be of no assistance (see below).

Careful consideration should always be given to identifying works within improvement schemes that are 'repair' works. Consultation may need to be obtained under section 20 of LTA 1985 on such works (see Chapter 5).

Nuisance and quiet enjoyment

Nuisance and harassment affect leaseholders in the same way as short-term residential tenants; see generally C. Hunter and K. Bretherton, *Anti-Social Behaviour* (Arden's Housing Library) forthcoming 1998.

Complaints by leaseholders

If a leaseholder has a complaint about the behaviour of another leaseholder or a tenant, there is a number of courses open to him or her.

Complaint to the landlord A landlord should have procedures for dealing with disputes between neighbours (sometimes the lease itself dictates a procedure, such as arbitration).

If after any such procedure the dispute is unresolved, the landlord can take legal action against the offending tenant or leaseholder under the relevant covenant in his or her lease. Sometimes a covenant in the complaining leaseholder's lease allows him or her to force the landlord to take legal action so long as the leaseholder repays the cost; however, a leaseholder may be loathe to pay for costs outside of his or her control.

Legal action by the leaseholder A leaseholder like any occupier of land can take action for tortious nuisance against the offending neighbour (for an injunction and damages). Criminal proceedings may be taken in the magistrates court under the Environmental Protection Act 1990 (see further, A. Hunter and K. Bretherton *Anti-Social Behaviour* (Arden's Housing Library) forthcoming 1998). Where restrictive covenants under a letting scheme allow, a leaseholder may be able to sue another for breach of covenant (see e.g. *Kelly v Battershell* (1949)). The rules for letting schemes are not discussed in this book.

Legal action against the landlord is unlikely to be a viable course. The covenant for quiet enjoyment in all leases covers the unlawful acts of the landlord and the lawful acts of tenants and leaseholders. It does not create liability for a nuisance caused by other tenants or leaseholders where the landlord is aware of it and takes no action. It is only in the rare case where the landlord 'authorises' the nuisance (that is, where the nuisance is the result of the tenant's or leaseholder's use of the premises in a normal manner for the purposes for which they were let) that the landlord may be liable under the covenant or generally in nuisance.

Complaints against leaseholders

Complaints against leaseholders (see above) may be dealt with by the landlord in accordance with the lease terms. The landlord may seek an injunction and damages or, in an extreme case, take forfeiture proceedings. The landlord need not take action unless the terms of the lease provide an obligation to do so.

Leases may usefully include a clause prohibiting nuisance and annoyance. The landlord can then decide what is or is not nuisance etc. (subject to the condition that the decision is *bona fide*). Such a clause can give an extended definition to include harassment (see further C. Hunter and K. Bretherton, *Anti-Social Behaviour* (Arden's Housing Library) forthcoming 1998).

Insurance

The landlord usually covenants to insure the block with reputable insurers and the leaseholder pays a portion of the insurance premiums as 'additional rent', through the service charge, or under a separate covenant.

The landlord has discretion over the choice of insurer and the insurance cost and is under no obligation, implied or specific, to keep insurance costs down (*Bandar v Darwen* (1968)). But there may be an express lease term for the landlord to insure at a reasonable cost (see further section 19 of LTA 1985 which applies to insurance costs recouped through a service charge).

Leaseholders' statutory insurance rights

Section 30A of and the Schedule to the LTA 1985 (as inserted by LTA 1987) set out a scheme of rights for leaseholders who contribute to insurance costs through a service charge.

A leaseholder (or 'recognised tenants' association' may require the landlord:

1. to provide a written summary of the insurance (or a copy of every relevant policy) within one month of a request to do so (paragraph 2)
2. within six months of receiving that summary, to permit inspection of the policy and other documents showing that the premium has been paid and to provide facilities for copying them (paragraph 3).

The inspection facilities must be available for a two-month period beginning not later than one month after the request is made. They must be free of charge at the time (they may be added later to the management costs), but a reasonable charge may be made for copying. These provisions also apply to superior landlords.

Failure to comply with these rules is a summary offence under paragraph 6 (but note that local authorities cannot be prosecuted – paragraph 9).

A leaseholder has the right to notify the insurers of a claim under paragraph 7. Where he or she must insure the flat with an insurer nominated by the landlord, he or she may challenge the landlord's choice in the county court or the LVT if it is unsatisfactory or the premiums are too high (but not where the matter has been agreed between the parties) (paragraph 8, as substituted by section 83(2) of HA 1996).

Any amount paid by the landlord over and above an insurance claim can be recovered through the service charge. If just one leaseholder was responsible for the claim being made, the landlord can recover the extra cost from that person only. For variation of the insurance covenant, see below.

Services

Where significant services are provided under the lease, such as in leasehold schemes for the elderly, care should be taken to draw up the list of services as clearly as possible.

The 'Advisory Note on Sheltered Housing' (House Builders Federation) outlines various matters that should be dealt with in leases for schemes for the elderly. In particular, provision of a resident warden and the services he or she is to perform should be specifically spelt out.

Assignment and subletting

At common law, the leaseholder is entitled to sublet the whole or part of the flat. Private landlords tend not to restrict this right because subletting is an important means available to the leaseholder of utilising the leasehold.

A lease may nevertheless absolutely prohibit subletting or permit it only with the landlord's prior consent. The latter type of covenant may additionally expressly stipulate that a landlord will not unreasonably withhold such consent to a sublet. If it does not, section 19(1) of LTA 1927 provides similarly, notwithstanding any provision to the contrary, that the landlord cannot unreasonably withhold consent to any subletting. The LTA 1988 deals with the procedure for applying for such a consent. Upon a leaseholder's written application for consent, it requires a landlord, within a reasonable time

1. to give consent, except where it is reasonable not to do so, and;
2. to serve on the leaseholder written notice of the decision whether or not to give consent.

The Act also provides remedies where the landlord seeks to delay the giving of consent.

Right to buy leases cannot prohibit or restrict subletting. But the sample leases issued by the Housing Corporation and Housing for Wales for shared ownership leases and leaseholds for the elderly do contain absolute prohibitions. It is however possible to apply to the Housing Corporation for a variation of the terms.

Assignment is dealt with in detail in Chapter 10.

Development

A compulsory purchase order must be obtained if the landlord wants to develop the property but the leaseholder refuses to sell up and move.

Variation of covenants

A lease term may need to be varied because it is defective, or it creates administrative difficulties because it differs from other lease agreements in a block, or simply it is old.

The lease may contain limited provision, either discretionary or by a set procedure, for the landlord to vary the services provided. But any other variation must be by agreement, drawn up in a deed, between the parties to the lease (and any mortgagee). If agreement cannot be reached, a party to a long lease can apply to the courts to order a variation (section 35 of LTA 1987). A 'long lease' is one exceeding 21 years, or which is perpetually renewable, or a right to buy lease (section 59). A lease for three or more flats in one block, a shared ownership lease and a section 149(6) of LPA 1925 lease are not long leases.

Application to vary individual lease

Either the landlord or the leaseholder may apply to the county court where the lease fails to make 'satisfactory provision' for:
- repair and maintenance
- insurance
- a reasonable standard of accommodation by maintaining and repairing installations such as lifts, and providing and maintaining services
- recovering costs incurred, and
- computing service charges.

It is for the court to decide (e.g. with expert evidence) whether a term is unsatisfactory. Failure to make satisfactory provision for computing the service charge is defined specifically in section 35(4). Under this section, the landlord is not entitled to require a leaseholder to pay more than the actual expenditure but is entitled to recoup that expenditure. The condition, safety and security of the flat and any common parts influence whether there is a 'reasonable standard of accommodation' (section 35(3)).

Cross applications

The unsatisfactory provision subject to variation may apply to other leases of properties belonging to the same landlord. An application can be made under section 36 for those leases to be varied to the same effect.

Grounds of opposition

A landlord or leaseholder can oppose a variation on grounds of substantial prejudice or unreasonableness.

Court orders

The court's power to make an order is discretionary. Orders that it can make are found in section 38. It cannot make an order which:
1. terminates any right of the landlord to nominate an insurer
2. requires the landlord to nominate a number of insurers from which the leaseholder can select an insurer
3. where a leaseholder is bound to insure with a specified insurer, requires the leaseholder to effect insurance with another insurer.

The order can provide for compensation to be paid for any loss or disadvantage that is likely to flow from the variation.

Application to vary several leases

Either a landlord or a number of leaseholders can make an application for the same variation of two or more leases (held by the same landlord but not necessarily in the same building) (section 37). This only applies where a variation to only one lease is ineffective without variation to the other lease. There must be majority leaseholder consent to the application, in that where there are:

1. less than nine leases, all but one party concerned must consent;
2. more than eight leases, at least 75 per cent of the parties concerned must consent, and no more than 10 per cent of them oppose it.

The landlord is treated as one of the parties concerned (section 37(6)(b)).

A section 37 variation is not limited to the 'unsatisfactory' matters listed in section 35. But the same grounds of opposition apply as for section 35 or 36 variations. A variation order under section 37 varies all the relevant leases (i.e. including those of any objecting leaseholders).

Variations to leases of dwellings other than flats

Such variations can be applied for, along the above lines, in connection only with the insurance provisions of the lease (section 40).

Regulation of management

There is a variety of ways in which leasehold properties can be managed. Social landlords often manage in house; private landlords often use managing agents. Whichever method is used, good management is characterised by diligent performance of the landlord's (or manager's) obligations and good value for the service charge paid. Managers may fall short of one or both of these goals, however, for a variety of reasons. In recent years, statutory mechanisms have been introduced to regulate the management of blocks of flats and the services provided.

Consultation and information rights

Section 30B of LTA 1985 gives 'recognised tenants' associations' (but not an individual leaseholder) consultation and information rights. 'Recognised tenants' association' is defined in Chapter 5.

The rights are initiated by the association serving a section 30B(1) notice on the landlord in connection with either the appointment or employment of managing agents. The association must then be provided with details of the managing agent and the obligations it is to discharge on the landlord's behalf. The landlord must take into account any responses subsequently received from the association. Once served with a section 30B(1) notice, the landlord is then bound every five years to inform the association of any changes in the agent's duties, and at any time when the landlord changes the agent. A fresh section 30B notice must be served on a new landlord.

Management audit

Sections 76-84 of LRHUDA 1993 gives qualifying tenants the right to a management audit to ascertain that:

1. the landlord's management obligations which have been discharged are being carried out efficiently and effectively; and
2. service charge payments are being applied efficiently and effectively.

The audit may be used as a prelude to appointment of a manager under section 24 of LTA 1987 (see Chapter 9).

'Qualifying tenants' are leaseholders with long leases

who pay service charges. A long lease is one exceeding 21 years; or which is perpetually renewable; or a section 149(6) LPA 1925 lease (see Chapter 1); or, a right to buy or rent to mortgage leasehold (see section 77).

The following may require an audit:

1. a single qualifying tenant, in which case it is carried out on his or her flat;
2. where there are two qualifying tenants, either or both of them; if only one requires it, only his or her flat is audited; if both require it, both flats are audited;
3. two-thirds of three or more qualifying tenants, in which case all their flats are audited.

The audit must include the block containing the flats and any other property managed under the lease agreement.

The right is exercised by serving a notice on the landlord (or on the person receiving rent on the landlord's behalf), signed on the participating leaseholders' behalf (section 80 of the 1993 Act). The notice must state:

- the leaseholders' names and addresses
- the auditor's name and address
- the documents the author wishes to see, and
- the date of any inspection proposed.

The landlord must comply with the notice within one month. An order can be obtained from the court under section 81 compelling the landlord to do so. These provisions apply to superior landlords under section 82.

The auditor may ask the landlord (or someone who has purchased the property from the landlord) for a LTA 1985 section 21 summary of relevant service charges (see Chapter 4) and permission to inspect supporting documents (section 79(2)). No charge may be made for providing facilities for inspection but a reasonable charge may be made for supplying and copying documents. Any costs incurred for providing facilities for inspection or copying may be recoverable as management costs through the service charge clause (section 79(6)).

Right to appoint a surveyor

Section 84 of the HA 1996 gives 'recognised tenants' associations' (see Chapter 5) (but not an individual leaseholder) a right to appoint a surveyor to advise on service charges. By such an appointment the association may investigate any matter relating to, or which may give rise to, service charges payable to the landlord.

The right is exercised by serving a written notice of the appointment on the landlord (or the person who receives rent on the landlord's behalf). The notice must state:
- the surveyor's name and address;
- the duration of his or her appointment; and
- the matters to be investigated.

The surveyor has a right to inspect relevant documents, and to inspect the premises. Inspection facilities must be given free of charge to the leaseholder (but may be added to management costs); a reasonable charge may be made for copying. The landlord (or any other person responsible for applying the service charge and/or for the works or services provided) must provide the facilities within one week or else give reasons for non-compliance. Compliance is enforceable by court proceedings. The same applies to superior landlords and to someone who has purchased the property from the landlord. For the detailed provisions, see Schedule 4 to HA 1996.

Key points

- For repair obligations, read the lease. Where there is a problem it may be possible to imply a term as to repair or obtain a court variation.
- For rights to alter or improve, leaseholders may be permitted to make minor alterations with the landlord's consent. The landlord may be permitted to alter and improve both the common parts of a block (in which access may be required through the leaseholder's flat, for which see

ATNLA 1992) and the leaseholder's flat (in which case the right must be reserved in the lease).

- If major works of repair and improvement are planned, section 20 LTA 1985 must be considered.
- As to nuisance, leaseholders are entitled to sue or to compel landlords to sue (if it is an express term of the lease). Save where they are required to sue (as above), landlords may choose whether to sue – seeking an injunction and damages, or forfeiture of the leasehold.
- Leaseholders may obtain information about the insurance under section 30A of LTA 1985.
- For service obligations, read the lease.
- The lease dictates whether subletting is permissible and/or whether the landlord's consent to sub-letting must first be sought.
- Variation of the covenants of a lease may be obtained:
  1. by a binding agreement with the other party to the lease;
  2. by a party to the lease under section 35 of LTA 1987 (regarding services, repairs, maintenance, insurance or service charge);
  3. as a consequence of a section 35 application, by the other party to the varied lease under section 36 seeking similar variations to other leases;
  4. by a party or parties seeking a similar variation of a number of leases under section 37 (regarding any matter in the lease).
- As to management generally:
  1. leaseholders' associations may obtain information, and make representations, about the appointment and employment of managing agents (section 30B of LTA 1985);
  2. leaseholders may require an audit in connection with the performance of the landlord's management obligations and the application of the service charge (LRHUDA 1993);
  3. leaseholders' associations may appoint a surveyor to advise on service charges (section 84 of HA 1996).

9.
Remedies of Landlord and Leaseholder

Forfeiture / Arrears of service charge and other sums / Tribunal appointed managers / Appointment of a receiver / Compulsory acquisition of reversion

Detailed discussion of the enforcement of covenants is beyond the scope of this book, but see A. Kilpatrick, *Repairs and Maintenance* (Arden's Housing Library) 1996 and C. Hunter and K. Bretherton, *Anti-Social Behaviour* (Arden's Housing Library) forthcoming 1998. Tortious actions by and against leaseholders are generally available in the same way as for short-term residential tenants.

The distinctive remedy of forfeiture, however, is covered in this chapter. It is the most draconian remedy that a landlord can use to enforce the covenants. A completed forfeiture terminates the leasehold before the term expires. A leaseholder who permits a forfeiture to occur therefore relinquishes his or her capital investment. Accordingly there is a great incentive for a leaseholder to comply with the covenants. Forfeiture is analogous to a landlord threatening a short-term residential tenant with possession proceedings.

Leaseholders (or other tenants), too, in certain circumstances, have draconian remedies against a landlord in breach of the landlord's covenants. These are also considered below.

Forfeiture

The conditions that entitle a landlord to forfeit the leasehold are that there must:
■ be a forfeiture clause; and
■ have been a breach of covenant which gives the landlord a right to forfeit the leasehold.

Waiver

A landlord must decide when a breach of covenant has been discovered whether to forfeit the leasehold. There are three situations. The landlord may:

1. immediately give a specific indication of an intention to forfeit the lease; or
2. immediately 'waive' the right to forfeit arising from the breach; or
3. wait and do nothing, before making a decision whether to forfeit or waive. This is an inadvisable course that risks a 'waiver' occuring.

'Waiver' is where the landlord, with knowledge of a breach that permits a forfeiture of the lease, does something unambiguous which is consistent only with the continued existence of the lease (e.g. accepting or demanding rent for some time after the breach has occurred). The landlord is thereafter prevented from reversing this course of action and attempting to forfeit. The danger for a landlord is that a waiver may in many circumstances (e.g. by accepting rent) arise quite inadvertently.

The effect of the doctrine of waiver is weakened by a distinction that has evolved between two types of breach of covenant. Breaches of covenant may be 'one-off' (because they can only be broken at one point in time, e.g. rent or service charge must be paid on a specified day), or 'continuing'. A continuing breach is one where there is a continuing duty on the leaseholder to either do something (e.g. repair) or not do something (e.g. not commit a nuisance) and by non-compliance with which the leaseholder continually breaches the covenant. An act of waiver waives both types of breach but a continuing breach, by its very nature, is likely to arise again in the future and so provide the landlord with a fresh right to forfeit. If a landlord is seriously considering forfeiting a leasehold, once notice is received of a breach of covenant, care must be taken not to waive the breach.

Restrictions on right to forfeit

The landlord must comply with legal restrictions on forfeiture.

Non-payment of rent

For non-payment of ground rent, or other sums 'reserved as if they were rent' or 'additional rent' (which expressions have the effect, for these purposes, of turning these sums into rent), there must be a formal demand for the rent unless this requirement has expressly been dispensed with in the lease or there is more than six months rent owing (Common Law Procedure Act 1852 and County Courts Act 1984). A 'formal demand' is defined by the common law in a highly technical way and if one is needed reference should be made either to specialist advice or to a specialist text on landlord and tenant law (e.g. *Woodfall on Landlord and Tenant*).

Leases should be read carefully to ascertain how insurance costs and service charges are payable by the leaseholder. If the wording treats them as 'reserved as if they were rent', forfeiture for non-payment must be preceded by a formal demand. This wording has other implications for the landlord on limitation of actions (and on distress, see Chapter 7). If, for instance, the service charge is 'reserved as if it was rent', proceedings for non-payment of it must be taken within six years of the right to payment arising. By contrast if the charge is payable under a covenant, the limitation period is twelve years.

Breaches of other covenants

For breach of any other covenants, the landlord must serve a section 146 (LPA 1925) notice on the leaseholder. This notice must:

- specify the breach complained of;
- if the breach can be remedied, require that it be remedied; and
- in any case, require the leaseholder to pay compensation for the breach.

Almost all breaches of covenant can be remedied as a matter of law (*Expert Clothing v Hillgate House* (1986)). A breach of a covenant not to use the flat for immoral or illegal purposes may give rise to an 'irremediable breach of covenant'. Section 146 notices carry further requirements when forfeiture is sought for breach of a leaseholder's repairing or service charge covenant (see below).

Effecting the forfeiture

If all the above are satisfied and the leaseholder remains in breach, the landlord may, ordinarily, forfeit by either commencing proceedings for forfeiture or re-taking physical possession of the premises.

Where the premises are occupied as a dwelling and someone is residing there, re-entry or forfeiture under the original lease is unlawful unless done so through court proceedings (section 2 of PEA 1977). It is good practice to effect forfeiture of any residential leasehold through the courts, irrespective of whether anyone presently resides there.

Relief from forfeiture

While issuing county court or High Court proceedings is a sufficient act of forfeiture, it does not necessarily forfeit the lease; the leaseholder is entitled to apply for relief from forfeiture.

If the matter arises because of non-payment of rent, the leaseholder must pay off all rent arrears and the court action costs before relief can be given. Where there is breach of other covenants, relief is usually granted under section 146 of LPA 1925, at the court's discretion, on the condition that the leaseholder remedies that and any other breach outstanding at the time of hearing. Each case turns on its own facts, however, and the court pays particular attention to the seriousness of the breach and the attitude of the parties.

Sub-leaseholders and mortgagees

Where a landlord successfully forfeits a leasehold, the leasehold is immediately brought to an end. Consequently, any sub-leaseholds in existence at that time are also terminated (because they are dependent on the leasehold's continued existence). A mortgagee of the leasehold loses his or her security.

For these reasons, relief from forfeiture is extended to sub-leaseholders and mortgagees (section 146(6)). Relief is granted upon remedying any relevant breaches of covenant.

Decorative repairs

If a section 146 notice is served in connection with internal decorative repairs to a 'house or a building' (or a flat), the leaseholder may apply to the court for relief (section 147). If, having regard to all the circumstances, the court is satisfied that the notice is unreasonable it may relieve the leaseholder, wholly or partially, from the liability to do the repairs (section 147 of LPA 1925).

Relief cannot be obtained where:
- an express covenant to put the property into a decorative state of repair has never been performed
- the repair is necessary or proper to put or keep the property in a sanitary condition, or to maintain or preserve the structure

- there is a statutory liability to keep a property in all respects reasonably fit for human habitation
- there is a covenant that the property must be in a specified state of repair at the end of the term.

Long leaseholders under LTA 1954

Part I of LTA 1954 and Sch.10 to LGHA 1989 provide specific protection for long leases where the landlord terminates by forfeiture (see Chapter 11).

Breach of leaseholder's repairing or service charge covenant

Repairs

A section 146 notice served because of a leaseholder's breach of a covenant to maintain or repair must clearly state, under Leasehold Property (Repairs) Act 1938:

- that the leaseholder may serve a counter-notice within 28 days of receiving the section 146 notice; and
- the name and address on which the counter-notice can be served.

Failure to do this makes the section 146 notice invalid.

A counter-notice served by a leaseholder within time stops the landlord taking forfeiture proceedings without the court's leave. The court may only grant leave in one of five situations, that is, where:

1. immediate repairs must be done to prevent a substantial drop in the premises' value, or the value has substantially dropped;
2. a repair must be done to comply with a statutory duty, by-law, court order or local authority notice;
3. an occupier is disadvantaged because repair is needed;
4. repair would be significantly cheaper now than if it is postponed; or
5. it is just and equitable that leave is given.

The LP(R)A 1938 applies to most leaseholds discussed in this book. Three exceptions worthy of note are where:
- the original lease term is less than seven years;
- less than three years of the lease term are unexpired at the date the notice is served; and
- a leaseholder breaches a covenant to repair the premises on taking possession or within a reasonable time thereafter.

Service charges

The Housing Act 1996 protects leaseholders where forfeiture for non-payment of service charges is contemplated. These provisions apply to all landlords of residential premises. They were introduced because some private stock landlords took forfeiture proceedings over disputed service charges to pressure leaseholders to accept disadvantageous settlements.

The bar on recovery The provisions are twofold. First, by section 81, no such forfeiture can be effected unless the service charge amount has been agreed, admitted or determined in court or by arbitration (an LVT decision does not amount to such a determination). If the amount has been determined, forfeiture may be exercised 14 days after the date of determination notwithstanding the possibility of an appeal.

Section 146 notice Despite the section 81 restriction, a landlord is still entitled to serve a section 146 notice (i.e. where the service charge is not reserved as rent) in anticipation of an agreement or determination. Under section 82, the notice must conspicuously state that section 81 applies and set out the effect of section 81(1) (section 82(3) and (4)). Failure to comply with these requirements renders the notice ineffective as far as failure to pay service charges is concerned.

Arrears of service charge and other sums

The point in time when service charges (or ground rent or sums due for insurance) become due and owing depends on the lease terms. Once due the landlord may issue proceedings for recovery.

Proceedings for the recovery of service charges are for a debt (not damages), whether the service charge is reserved as rent or not (for the importance of this distinction for distress (see Chapter 7) and for forfeiture and limitation (see above).

A leaseholder with a claim against the landlord, say for damages for disrepair, may be able to set off the sums due under that claim against the landlord's claim. But not if there is a lease term that clearly prohibits any set-off from the service charge (or ground rent).

Interest may be claimed on arrears if there is a lease term providing for interest. Otherwise, once proceedings are issued, interest may be claimed under Supreme Court Act 1981 or County Courts Act 1984.

Restrictions

Two statutory provisions impose information requirements on landlords which, if not complied with, treat these arrears as not having fallen due. These provisions apply when the landlord is simply suing for arrears and also for other purposes (e.g. if the landlord is seeking forfeiture for non-payment of rent or distress).

Section 47 of LTA 1987

This section (which applies to all residential leases that do not involve business use) requires that any demand for rent or other sums such as service charges must contain:
- the landlord's name and address; and
- if that address is not in England and Wales, an address

in England and Wales at which notices (including notices in proceedings) can be served on the landlord by the leaseholder.

Failure to comply with this section means that any part of the amount demanded which consists of service charge within the statutory class (see section 18 of LTA 1985) is to be treated as not being due from the leaseholder until compliance takes place.

Section 48 of LTA 1987

This section, additionally, requires that a landlord must by notice provide the leaseholder with an address in England and Wales at which the leaseholder may serve notices (including notices in proceedings). Failure to comply results in rent or service charges not being due, in the same way as for section 47 above.

The effect of section 48 is not to make the rent or charges irrecoverable – a notice can always be served to render them recoverable. But the section can cause administrative problems; it is argued that litigation commenced before compliance with section 48 is invalid. This may result in costs consequences for the landlord.

> **Case Report**
>
> In *Rogan v Woodfield Building Services* (1994), the Court of Appeal held that the section 48 requirements are satisfied when the landlord's address is contained within the lease itself (although notice may be provided otherwise). However, that will not suffice where there has been an assignment of the reversion and there is a new landlord, in which case the new landlord must serve a notice on the leaseholder. Further, it is not clear whether the section is complied with if the present landlord has (inadvertently) provided the leaseholder with several addresses. Ideally therefore, a formal notice expressly served under section 48 should be served on a leaseholder to ensure compliance with the section.

Tribunal appointed managers

Under Part II of LTA 1987 (as amended by sections 85-87 of and Schedule 5 to HA 1996), the LVT has power to appoint a manager over a building comprising of two or more dwellings (section 21).

Exemptions

The provisions do not apply if there is an exempt landlord (e.g. a local authority, a registered housing association or an unregistered, fully mutual housing association) or a resident landlord (i.e. who lives in a flat on the premises as his or her only or principal residence for at least a 12-month period and the premises are not a purpose built block of flats) (section 58 of LTA 1987).

Procedure

Under section 22, the leaseholder serves a preliminary notice on the landlord which must state the breaches of covenant complained of and that these must be remedied within a reasonable period. The notice can be dispensed with if the landlord cannot be served. An order appointing a manager can be granted on the following grounds when it is just and convenient to do so:

1. the landlord is in breach of a management obligation, or
2. unreasonable service charges have been made or are proposed, or
3. the landlord has failed to comply with a code of practice under section 87 of LRHDA 1993 (for examples, see Chapter 2), or
4. other circumstances exist (e.g. the landlord has disappeared).

A service charge is unreasonable if the items are:

- not worth the amount demanded;
- of an unnecessarily high standard; or

- of insufficient standard resulting in additional charges possibly or actually being made.

There are detailed rules governing LVT applications and fees (sections 24A and 24B); these are similar to the rules for section 19 disputes (see Chapter 4).

Appointment of a receiver

A receiver may be appointed by the court over property managed by housing associations (but not local authorities – see *Parker v Camden London Borough Council* (1985)) under the general provisions of section 37 of the Supreme Court Act 1981 whenever it is just and equitable to do so (see A. Kilpatrick, *Repairs and Maintenance* (Arden's Housing Library) 1996, Ch. 5).

Compulsory acquisition of reversion

Some leaseholders have the right to compulsorily acquire their leaseholder's interest under Part III of LTA 1987 (as amended by LRHUDA 1993 and section 88 of HA 1988) 'where there has been a problem with the landlord's management'. The block must contain two or more flats held by qualifying tenants; at least two-thirds of the flats in the block must be held by such tenants (section 25). Application for an acquisition must be made by at least two-thirds of the qualifying tenants on a one-vote-per-flat basis (section 27). A qualifying tenant for these purposes does not include one who owns the leasehold to at least two other flats, or whose landlord is a qualifying tenant (section 26).

Exemptions

The provisions do not apply if there is an exempt or a resident landlord (see above). Nor do they apply where more than 50 per cent of the internal floor area (excluding common parts) is occupied otherwise than for residential purposes (section 25).

Procedure

The tenant serves a preliminary notice on the landlord which specifies the particular breaches of covenant complained of and requiring remedy of them within a reasonable period of time (section 27). The grounds upon which an acquisition order may be made are that:

- the landlord is in breach of an obligation to repair, maintain, insure or manage the premises, and the breaches are likely to continue, or alternatively,
- an appointed manager has been in place for at least two years.

If after a reasonable time the breaches have not been remedied, or are incapable of remedy (e.g. because of failure to insure), or the notice is dispensed with, the tenant may apply for an order. The procedure for making an acquisition order is governed by sections 30 and 31. If an order is made, the transferee of the reversion is a person nominated by the leaseholders (section 30); in the absence of agreement, determination of the terms (including the purchase price) is made by a rent assessment committee (section 31). The computation of the price under section 31 is favourable to the leaseholders by comparison with the price payable on collective enfranchisement under LRHUDA 1993. Provision is made in section 33 for acquisition where the landlord cannot be found.

Key points

- A landlord may terminate the leasehold by forfeiture where the leaseholder is in breach of covenant if:

- any procedural requirements on effecting forfeiture are complied with (i.e. formal demands and section 146 notices containing the correct information);
- there is no waiver by the landlord; and,
- the leaseholder fails to obtain relief from the court.
■ Before suing for arrears of rent, insurance sums and/or service charge, check for compliance with sections 47 and 48 of LTA 1987.
■ Leaseholders of housing associations may be able to obtain the appointment of a receiver where the landlord is in serious breach of management obligations.
■ Leaseholders of private landlords may be able to: obtain the appointment of a manager under Pt II of LTA 1985; or, compulsorily acquire the landlord's reversion under Pt III of LTA 1985 or a receiver, where the landlord is in serious breach of management obligations.

10.
Change of Leaseholder or Landlord

Change of leaseholder / Leaseholder
difficulties / Change of landlord

This chapter covers in detail the assignment of the leasehold by the leaseholder. The right to assign is fundamental to the ownership of the leasehold although for leaseholders of social landlords there may be certain restrictions on it (see the examples in Chapter 2). Some leaseholders, particularly right to buy leaseholders buying into high-rise blocks of flats or blocks with high maintenance charges, have recently found difficulty in selling on, either because their flats are unattractive to purchasers or because would-be purchasers have been unable to obtain mortgage finance. Measures introduced to alleviate this problem are considered below.

The chapter also considers succession and the assignment of the reversion by the landlord.

Change of leaseholder

Assignment: generally

The effect of an assignment is to transfer the leasehold to the new owner. This is so even if the assignment is in breach of a covenant against assignment (see below).

All assignments should be effected by deed (section 52 of LPA 1925) or, for registered land, by transfer registered at the Land Registry. An effective assignment transfers the 'legal estate' to the new owner ('the assignee'). If the assignment is not done by deed (or registered), the assignee takes only an 'equitable' leasehold and this does not create 'privity of estate' (see below) between the landlord and the assignee. In such a situation, the landlord may have problems attempting to enforce the covenants directly against the assignee.

Covenants concerning assignment

Covenant against assignment

By contrast with secure tenancies, under the common law if there is no provision to the contrary in the lease, the leaseholder is entitled to assign the leasehold in any way.

Covenants restricting assignment are uncommon. Those that do are likely to require that the landlord's consent is obtained before assignment. If so, as for subletting (see Chapter 8), section 19 of LTA 1927 provides, notwithstanding any provision to the contrary, that the landlord cannot unreasonably withhold consent to the assignment. The LTA 1988 requires the landlord to inform the leaseholder of the decision within a reasonable time. Assignment in breach of a restriction will entitle the landlord to forfeit.

Notification of assignment

A common lease covenant is that the leaseholder, shortly after the date of an assignment, gives written notice of it to the landlord. This covenant is included to give the landlord notice of the assignment within a reasonable time. The leaseholder is often required to pay a fee for the landlord's administrative costs in dealing with the notice.

This covenant alone is rather unreliable for recording changes in the ownership of the leasehold (note that a landlord who suffers loss by the assignee's failure to comply with this requirement can sue that person). Therefore landlords of a registered leasehold sometimes further place a restriction on the land register to prevent assignment without the landlord's consent.

Once a landlord becomes aware of an assignment, notices and demands should be sent to the assignee and compliance with sections 47 and 48 of LTA 1987 (chapter 9) should be checked.

Enforceability of covenants

There are now two sets of rules concerning the enforceability of covenants after a leasehold (or reversion, see below) has been assigned. The rules turn on the date when the leasehold was granted.

Leaseholds granted before 1 January 1996

The original leaseholder In circumstances where an original leaseholder (the one to whom the lease was originally granted) assigns the leasehold to another, the original leaseholder is divested of the legal estate. But his or her contractual liability to the landlord remains unaffected unless the original leaseholder and landlord have agreed otherwise. Therefore, in general, the original leaseholder remains liable on all the covenants throughout the term (this is called 'privity of contract').

This rule has come to be perceived as unfair or harsh. It means that an original leaseholder's contractual liability makes him or her liable for breaches of covenant after assignment. If sued for post-assignment breaches of covenant, the original leaseholder has a right of redress against the assignee or any subsequent owner of the leasehold (if different).

Since the introduction of the Landlord and Tenant (Covenants) Act 1995, however, original leaseholders are not liable for any subsequent leaseholder failing to pay a 'fixed charge' (which includes ground rent and service charges) unless the landlord has taken certain steps (see section 17). In brief, the landlord must serve a prescribed notice on the original leaseholder informing him or her that the landlord may seek to recover the fixed charge from the leaseholder. Such notices must be served within six months of any fixed charge item arising and, in connection with those fixed charges arising before 1 January 1996, before 30 June 1996.

Assignees On an assignment of the lease by the original leaseholder, the entitlement of the assignee of the term to enforce the covenants and the assignee's liability to observe the leaseholders' covenants derive from the doctrine of privity of estate (*Spencer's case* (1583)). Privity of estate means that the parties are in the position of landlord and leaseholder to each other.

Under this doctrine only covenants that affect the land (i.e. all those common covenants discussed in Chapter 2) can be enforced between landlord and assignee. The entitlement and liability only exist for the period of time during which there is privity of estate.

Accordingly an assignee is entitled to take action, or is liable, for breaches of covenant committed, by the landlord or himself or herself respectively, while the assignee owns the leasehold. The assignee is not liable for breaches occurring before the assignment to him or her.

> **Example**
>
> In December 1990, a local authority granted a right to buy leasehold to Mr Smith. In March 1994 Mr Smith assigned the leasehold to Mrs Brown. Mr Smith failed to pay the service charge from 1992 and there were arrears of £2,000 at the time of the assignment to Mrs Brown. Mrs Brown herself has failed to pay £3,000 worth of service charges since the assignment.

The local authority can sue Mr Smith for: his arrears of £2,000; and, the arrears of £3,000 if Mr Smith has been served with appropriate notice under section 17 of LT(C)A 1995. Mrs Brown can only be sued for her arrears of £3,000.

(Note that where the service charge is reserved as if it was rent, the arrears will be calculated by apportioning the first service charge between Mr Smith and Mrs Brown. Where there is no such covenant, the arrears will be all payments of service charge that fell due after the assignment in 1994, i.e. with no apportionment).

If there is no dispute as to the quantification of the arrears of service charge and there has been no waiver (see Chapter 9), the local authority can forfeit the leasehold for non-payment of the service charge. To obtain relief from forfeiture Mrs Brown will have to pay all the arrears of service charge.

Leaseholds granted after 1 January 1996

The LT(C)A 1995 has re-cast the law of enforceability of covenants for leaseholds granted after 1 January 1996. In outline, for residential leaseholders, the following points are of note:

- privity of contract has been abolished – once a leasehold is assigned the original leaseholder is no longer liable for post-assignment breaches of covenant;
- privity of estate has been abolished – one consequence of this is that an assignee of the leasehold becomes liable to perform all the covenants in the lease – another consequence is that previous difficulties of enforcement against an 'equitable' leaseholder are now overcome.

The position of all leaseholders after LT(C)A 1995 is now similar to that of assignees under the old rules: a leaseholder is entitled to take action, or is liable, for breaches of covenant committed, by the landlord or himself or herself respectively, while the leaseholder owns the leasehold.

Right to buy leases: repayment of discount

One of the most important right to buy lease covenants is to repay the discount, or a proportion of it, if there is a relevant disposal which is not exempt within three years of the purchase (section 155 of HA 1985). Note that the amount of discount repayable has changed through the legislation since 1980. Otherwise, right to buy leases may not restrict assignment (or sub-letting). These covenants are considered in Chapter 2 and in detail in J. Henderson, *Rights to Buy and Acquire* (Arden's Housing Library) 1997, Ch. 6.

Shared ownership leases

These will commonly contain provisions for assignment. If the lease permits 'staircasing' (see Chapter 1), the leaseholder can staircase to 100 per cent and thereafter freely assign the flat. If the leaseholder cannot staircase, there may be restrictions on the amount that the leasehold can be sold for and the persons to whom it may be sold. In non-staircasing shared ownership leaseholds, the landlord is likely to retain a right of pre-emption so that recovery can be made of the leasehold if the leaseholder wishes to sell (thereby preserving the flat for the type of person for whom the shared ownership scheme was set up).

Similarly leasehold schemes for the elderly commonly restrict assignment to elderly people.

Succession

A leasehold is inheritable property and, upon the death of the leaseholder, the relevant property will pass according to the will or rules of intestacy. By contrast with short term residential tenancies, there is no system of statutory succession for leaseholds.

Leaseholder difficulties

A large number of right to buy leaseholders have experienced difficulties in selling their flats. Measures have
been introduced which allow local authorities to address
this problem.

Assistance with mortgages

Under section 435 of HA 1985, local authorities can offer
mortgages to assist in buying, converting, repairing and
improving a flat, or for repaying a loan which was taken out
for these purposes. But local authority mortgages usually
charge higher than average interest rates and so have proved
to be unpopular.

Mortgage indemnities

Alternatively, under section 442 of the HA 1985 (as amended
by HA 1996), a local authority can enter into an agreement
with a commercial lender which has given a mortgage to a
leaseholder for any of the purposes outlined above. If the
leaseholder defaults, the authority can agree to indemnify
the lender (i.e. ensure that it is not out of pocket) for the
whole or part of the outstanding mortgage and any other
losses relating to it. It is also possible for the mortgage to be
transferred in full, at the authority's or the lender's request,
to the local authority, thus removing the commercial lender
from the mortgage arrangement.

   The provision allows a local authority to encourage a
commercial lender to grant a mortgage to a secure tenant
looking to buy his or her council flat, or a prospective buyer
from a right to buy leaseholder. This may in turn support a
fledgling market in properties many commercial lenders
would refuse to mortgage, and promote the recent policy
drive towards home ownership generally. A DoE guide
(September 1996) estimates that over the last ten years, only

three per cent of agreements have been invoked by lenders.

Before the HA 1996 amendments, the Secretary of State specified the type of indemnity agreement to be used, which had to be made with a building society or a recognised body. Local authorities can now agree terms as considered appropriate in each case with any commercial lender. A number of model agreements were produced under the old provisions; the model standard form of agreement was revised in June 1995 and is reproduced in the September 1996 DoE guidance.

Exchange sale scheme

The aim of this scheme is to assist leaseholders who are trying to sell unmortgageable flats (e.g. because of high service charges) (Part II of HA 1985 and Part IV of the Local Government Housing Act (LGHA) 1989). The leaseholder sells his or her flat back to the local authority at the original discounted price paid for it, and then buys another flat from the authority. There is a financial concession to encourage authorities to enter the scheme (see DoE general letter of assistance, 19 June 1995).

The following conditions must be met under regulation 104 of the Local Authorities (Capital Finance) Regulations 1997 to qualify for the scheme:

1. The leaseholder was the flat's former tenant (i.e. the person who acquired the leasehold or a successor through an exempt disposal under right to buy provisions).
2. The flat was acquired under a right to buy or by the authority's voluntary powers of disposal under section 32 or 42 of HA 1985, at a discount of at least 44 per cent of the market value.
3. The leasehold has been held for at least three years.
4. The leaseholder has occupied the flat as his or her only or principal home.
5. The authority must be satisfied that any person wishing to buy the relevant lease would be unlikely – for

reasons which do not relate to the personal or financial status of that person, or the terms of that lease, or the condition of the flat or building in which the flat is situated – to obtain from a lending institution an advance:

(a) secured by a mortgage of the relevant lease for a term of 25 years, and

(b) of an amount equal to 75 per cent of the value of that lease determined, not more than three months before the date of disposal, on the basis that there would be sale on the open market with any criteria which lending institutions might apply as to the height of blocks or numbers of owners in them being inapplicable.

6. The disposal is of:

(a) the freehold;

(b) the leasehold with at least 99 years of its term unexpired, and which the authority expects to receive at least 90 per cent of its capital value within one year after the date of disposal; or

(c) the assignment of the authority's leasehold interest in the flat.

7. The leaseholder assigns or surrenders the leasehold to the authority as part of the authority's consideration for the disposal.

Although not obliged to do so, an authority may offer a discount (up to 40 per cent for a flat, or 30 per cent for a new house or flat) when the leaseholder buys another property from it.

Change of landlord

Enforceability of covenants

For leaseholds granted before 1 January 1996, the new landlord of the reversion is not liable for breaches of covenant committed by the previous landlord before assignment. However, the new landlord is entitled to sue the leaseholder for breaches committed by him or her that occurred before the assignment (section 141 of LPA 1925).

For leaseholds granted after 1 January 1996, under LT(C)A 1995 a new landlord of the reversion is entitled to enforce, and is bound by, the covenants during ownership of the reversion. A new landlord cannot enforce, and is not liable for, pre-assignment breaches committed by the lease-holder or previous landlord respectively.

Landlord's name and address

Several statutory rules provide for leaseholders' rights to know their landlord's identity.

Landlord and Tenant Act 1985

On written request by the leaseholder, the landlord's rent collector or agent must disclose the landlord's name and address; where the landlord is a company, on further request the agent must disclose the name and address of the sec-retary and the director (sections 1 and 2). If the reversion is transferred the new landlord must notify the leaseholder in writing, giving his name and address, within two months from the transfer or by the next rent day, whichever is later (section 3). Failure to comply with these rules is a summary offence.

Additionally, on a transfer of the reversion, the former landlord remains liable (additional to any liability of the new landlord) under the covenants until written notice of the transfer giving the new landlord's name and address has been given to the leaseholder (section 3(3A)).

Landlord and Tenant Act 1987

Sections 47 and 48 of this Act provide further incentive to a landlord to inform a leaseholder of any transfer of the reversion (see Chapter 9 above).

Key points

- An assignment by the original leasehold owner transfers the leasehold to the assignee even if it is done in breach of covenant.
- If a leasehold is granted before 1 January 1996, unless agreed otherwise, the original lease-holder remains liable on the covenants for the whole lease term.
- However, an original leaseholder is not liable for any subsequent leaseholder failing to pay a fixed charge unless the landlord has served a section 17 prescribed notice on him within the relevant time period.
- Assignees are only liable for breaches of covenant that affect the land committed while they own the leasehold.
- If a leasehold is granted after 1 January 1996, all owners of the leasehold (original or assignee) are entitled to take action, or are liable, for breaches of covenant committed, by the landlord or themselves respectively, while they own the leasehold.
- If a leasehold is granted before 1 January 1996, a new landlord is not liable for breaches of covenant committed by the previous landlord but is entitled to sue the leaseholder for breaches committed by him or her before the assignment (section 141 of LPA 1925).
- If a leasehold is granted after 1 January 1996, a new landlord is only entitled to enforce, and is only liable under, the covenants during that landlord's ownership of the reversion.
- Assignment of a right to buy leasehold may require the original leaseholder to repay some of the discount. Shared ownership leaseholds commonly contain restrictions on assignment.
- Leaseholders owning flats they wish to sell, but on which mortgagees are unwilling to lend to purchasers, may be assisted by a local authority entering into a mortgage indemnity agreement with a purchaser's mortgagee or purchasing the property under the exchange sale scheme.

- A leaseholder is entitled to know the name and address of the landlord (see generally section 1-3 of LTA 1985 and sections 47 and 48 of LTA 1987).

11.
Security of tenure

Housing Act 1988 / Schedule 10 to LGHA 1989

Short term tenants who fall within the Rent Act (RA) 1977 or the Housing Acts (HA) 1985 or 1988 are not limited to the period of occupation that is set out in their contractual tenancy. These statutes extend their rights of occupation and termination is permitted only in specific statutory circumstances. This reflects a policy that seeks to promote the security of residential occupiers. Although most long leaseholders of social landlords have many years to run on their leaseholds, eventually such leaseholders will reach the end of their term. Are they entitled to similar extended rights of occupation?

The above mentioned Acts exclude leaseholders because of 'low rent' and 'long tenancy' exceptions (see generally, A. Dymond *Security of Tenure* (Arden's Housing Library) 1996). Instead, leaseholders have had to rely on Part I of the LTA 1954. Leaseholds falling within this Act are, once the expiry date passes, continued automatically until terminated in accordance with provisions of the Act. In these circumstances similar security to that enjoyed by short term tenants is provided to leaseholders.

The LTA 1954 provides security to long tenancies at a low rent which satisfy the qualifying condition. The words 'long tenancy', 'at a low rent' and 'qualifying condition' have special technical meanings (these meanings are discussed later in this Chapter under the similar definition in section 186 of and Schedule 10 to LGHA 1989. For the moment, it is the last of these that is important. Under LTA 1954, the qualifying condition invites consideration of a hypothetical situation. To benefit from the statute, the lease-holder's occupation must be such that if the leasehold had not been one within the RA 1977 low rent exception, on the coming to an end of the leasehold the leaseholder would have qualified for protection under the RA 1977. This there-fore requires that:

- the premises must be let as a separate dwelling
- they must be occupied by the leaseholder as his or her residence; and
- none of the other exceptions in sections 4 to 16 of RA 1977 apply (see generally A. Dymond, *Security of Tenure* (Arden's Housing Library) 1995.

For leaseholders of private landlords, this is often a straight-forward matter; but leaseholders of social landlords are in a different position. Sections 14 and 15 of RA 1977 exclude tenants of local authorities and (most) housing associations from the ambit of RA 1977. (Such tenants were in the early 1980s covered by a completely different system under the HA 1985.) Accordingly, leaseholders of social landlords (save those housing associations not excepted from the RA 1977) cannot satisfy the qualifying condition of LTA 1954.

Housing Act 1988

The HA 1988 introduced a new system for the regulation of short term tenancies – the 'assured tenancy' system. This system differed significantly from that governed by the RA 1977 and, as part of the general operation of the HA 1988, it provided (subject to some exceptions) that no new RA 1977 tenancies could be created after the HA 1988 came into force on 15 January 1989. The unintended consequence was that the combination of this provision of the HA 1988 and the provisions of Part I of LTA 1954 prevented leaseholders from satisfying the qualifying condition of the 1954 Act if their leaseholds were granted after 15 January 1989. Given the veto on the creation of RA 1977 tenancies after this date, no leaseholder whose leasehold was entered into after this date could ever qualify for protection under RA 1977 (and thereby satisfy the qualifying condition of the 1954 Act).

Section 186 and Schedule 10 to the LGHA 1989 remedied the above problem. Rather than amending the 1954 Act, this section and Schedule introduced a new scheme, similar to but distinct from the 1954 Act, for the protection of leaseholders who acquire their leasehold after 1 April 1990 (it is discussed below). This scheme introduces a qualifying condition that is appropriate in the aftermath of the HA 1988. Now a leaseholder is protected if the circumstances of the leaseholder's occupation of the property are such that if the leasehold had not been one within the HA 1988 low rent exception, on the ending of the leasehold the leaseholder would have qualified for protection under HA 1988.

It appears that leaseholds that have been created between 15 January 1989 and 1 April 1990 do not qualify for protection under either Act. This odd result is unlikely to affect many leaseholders and the problem will not arise for some time. It is thought that the courts will strive hard to construe the relevant Acts so as to give such leaseholders some protection. (Leaseholds which are governed by the 1954 Act, i.e. those granted before 15 January 1989, and are in existence on 15 January 1999 will (subject to a few exceptions) after that date, be governed by the rules of the 1989 Act).

Schedule 10 to LGHA 1989

The 1989 Act provides long tenancy, low rent leaseholders with security of tenure if they satisfy the qualifying condition of the 1989 Act. Leaseholds that fall within the 1989 Act are, once the expiry date passes, continued automatically terminated in accordance with the provisions of the 1989 Act.

The 1989 Act applies to leaseholds entered into either:
- after 30 March 1990 (and possibly also those after 15 January 1989); and
- before those dates but phased out after 15 January 1999 (section 186(3) of LGHA 1989).

A 'long tenancy' means a leasehold exceeding 21 years but not if terminated by notice given to the leaseholder before the term date. Where on the coming to an end of a long tenancy at a low rent within the above definition a second tenancy or leasehold (including a periodic tenancy) is granted to the leaseholder it is deemed to be a long tenancy.

Rent (as in the expression 'at a low rent') refers to 'pure' or ground rent (and not to, for example, service charges 'reserved as rent'). If the lease was entered into prior to 1 April 1990, the rent must be less than two-thirds of rateable value of the property on the appropriate day. Where the lease is entered into after 1 April 1990, the rent must be £1,000 per annum or less (for Greater London) or £250 per annum or less (elsewhere).

As stated above, the qualifying condition requires that, if the leasehold had not been one within the HA 1988 the low rent exception, on the coming to an end of the leasehold the leaseholder would have qualified for protection under the HA 1988. This raises an important distinction between the 1954 and 1989 Acts. While paragraph 12 of Schedule 1 to the HA 1988 excludes tenants of local authorities from HA 1988 protection, there is no exclusion for tenants of housing associations. Tenants of housing associations are assured tenants. Accordingly, leaseholders of local authorities cannot satisfy the qualifying condition of LTA 1954 but leaseholders of housing associations can.

Security of tenure before expiry

Before the expiry of the term, the leasehold may be terminated by exercising a leaseholder's break clause, or by surrender or forfeiture.

Where, before a 1989 Act leasehold expires, a landlord takes forfeiture proceedings upon a leaseholder's breach of covenant, the leaseholder may apply for relief (Schedule 10, paragraph 20, applying section 16 of LTA 1954) additional to that available generally (this is not discussed in detail in this book).

Security of tenure after expiry

Once the term date has passed, Schedule 10, paragraph 3 automatically continues the leasehold. Thereafter the tenancy may:

- run indefinitely;
- be terminated by the leaseholder;
- be converted into a assured periodic tenancy by the landlord; or
- be terminated by the landlord.

The tenancy may be terminated by the leaseholder by surrendering to the landlord or by at least one month's notice in writing (Schedule 10, paragraph 8).

Conversion or termination by landlord

The landlord may give notice to the leaseholder specifying a date (between 6 and 12 months from service) on which the tenancy is to come to an end (Schedule 10, paragraph 4). This notice may take one of two forms.

The notice may ask the leaseholder whether he or she wishes to remain in possession and contain proposals for the leaseholder to take an assured periodic tenancy (including terms, e.g. as to rent and repairs). In these circumstances, broadly, an assured periodic tenancy is likely to arise. This tenancy will only come to an end if the (now) tenant ceases to occupy the flat as his or her only or principle home or the landlord proves a HA 1988 ground of possession.

Alternatively, the notice will ask whether the leaseholder is willing to give up possession and state that, if he or she is not, the landlord will seek possession of the premises on one or more specified statutory grounds of possession. In this case, where the leaseholder elects, within time, to retain possession or fulfils the qualifying condition two months after service, the landlord will be entitled and forced to take proceedings for possession between two and four months from the service of the notices (Schedule 10, paragraph 13).

The landlord's proceedings for possession must be based on one of the following statutory grounds of possession:

Mandatory grounds of possession
- Ground 6, Schedule 2 of HA 1988 (demolition or reconstruction of the whole or a substantial part of the dwelling-house, see A. Dymond, *Security of Tenure* (Arden's Housing Library) 1995). This ground is not available where the leasehold was formerly within the 1954 Act (Schedule 10 paragraph 5(2)).
- For the purpose of redeveloping the property after the termination of the leasehold, the landlord proposes to demolish or reconstruct the whole or a substantial part of the premises (Schedule 10, paragraphs 5(1),(4),13(7)). This ground is only available to local authorities (or other landlords within section 28(5) of LRA 1967 – the list does not include housing associations).

Discretionary grounds of possession
- Grounds 9 to 15 in Schedule 2 of HA 1988 (not ground 16 – termination of tenant's employment) (Schedule 10, paragraph 5(1), see A. Dymond, *Security of Tenure* (Arden's Housing Library) 1995).
- The premises are reasonably required by the landlord as a personal residence or for certain members of the family (Schedule 10, paragraph 5(1),(5)). The ground does not apply where the landlord's interest was created or purchased after 1966.

If the landlord fails to apply to court in time or does not

succeed in proving a ground of possession, the continuation tenancy continues on.

Key points

- Long tenancy, low rent leaseholders with local authority and housing association landlords cannot qualify for protection under Pt I of LTA 1954.
- Long tenancy, low rent leaseholders with leaseholds created after 30 March 1990 (and probably after 15 January 1989) may be protected under Schedule 10 of LGHA 1989. If such leaseholders have local authority landlords they cannot obtain this protection.
- The effect of protection under Schedule 10 of LGHA 1989 is, after the expiry date of the leasehold, to continue the leasehold indefinitely unless it is: terminated by the leaseholder; terminated by the landlord on one of the specific statutory grounds; or converted into an assured periodic tenancy.

12.
Enfranchisement and Extension of Long Leases

Houses / Flats

Houses

The Leasehold Reform Act (LRA) 1967 confers on lease-holders occupying a house, but not a flat, the right to purchase their freehold ('enfranchise'), or to extend their leasehold for 50 years, 'on fair terms'. The Act is extended by the LRHUDA 1993 to enable some leaseholders who were previously excluded by the qualifying conditions to take advantage of the enfranchisement provisions.

Qualifying conditions

The following conditions must be met under section 1(1):
1. the leaseholder occupies the house as his or her residence;
2. the leasehold is a long, low rent tenancy;
3. the house is not high in value; and
4. at the time a section 5 notice is served (see below), the leaseholder has resided at the house for at least three years, or for short periods totalling at least three years, or for short periods totalling at least three years in the last ten years.

A 'house'

There is no absolute definition of a 'house' in the Act but, by section 2, 'a house' includes any building adapted or designed for living in. A building that is horizontally divided into flats may be a house, but the flats are not. A building that is vertically divided into living units is not a house, but the individual units may be. The building need not be used or adapted exclusively for residential purposes; therefore a shop with living accommodation above is often a house. Ultimately it is a question of fact whether a building is a house.

The residence requirements Under qualifying condition 4. above, the house must have been occupied, even if only in part, as the leaseholder's only or principal residence (see further A. Dymond, *Security of Tenure* (Arden's Housing Library) 1995). If the leaseholder dies, any successor who lived with him or her can count the period of time they lived together as part of the three-year period requirement (section 7).

Long tenancy This means a term certain exceeding 21 years (whether there is a break clause or not), including a new leasehold arising on the termination of a long, low rent tenancy, or a new leasehold granted pursuant to an option to renew (without payment of a further premium) where the totality of the terms granted exceeds 21 years (section 3).

Low rent

The test for 'low rent' differs according to when the lease was entered into (section 4).

In outline, for a lease entered into on or after 1 April 1990, the annual rent must not exceed £1,000 (Greater London) or £250 (elsewhere). For a lease entered into before that date, the annual rent must be not more than two-thirds of the property's rateable value on the appropriate day (or if later, the first day of the term). The 'appropriate day' is taken as 23 March 1965, or, if later, the date on which a figure for the property's rateable value first appeared on the valuation list. For leases entered into between 31 August 1939 and 1 April 1963, the rent must not exceed two-thirds of the property's letting value. For these purposes rent means 'pure' rent (not insurance or a service charge). Amendments introduced by HA 1996 now ensure that houses which had no rateable value at the date of letting may satisfy this requirement (see section 105 of HA 1996).

A leasehold exceeding 35 years does not need to satisfy the low rent test (section 1AA, as inserted by HA 1996). Such leaseholds include perpetually renewable and section 149(6) (LPA 1925) leaseholds, but not those in rural areas. Accordingly, only leaseholds of between 21 and 35 years length will need to satisfy the low rent requirement.

Low rent: enfranchisement Another type of low rent test exists under section 4A where the leaseholder seeks to enfranchise and not to extend the lease. The conditions are that either no rent was payable for the first year of the tenancy, or the rent did not exceed, for a lease entered into

- before 1 April 1963, two-thirds of the property's open market letting value on the date the tenancy commences;
- between 1 April 1963 and 1 April 1990, two-thirds of the property's rateable value on the first day of the term, or if later the first day the property had a rateable value; or
- on or after 1 April 1990, £1,000 in Greater London, or £250 elsewhere.

High value properties

By virtue of a number of complex provisions, a house may fall outside the 1967 Act scheme because it exceeds certain rateable values and rent limits set out in section 1(1)(a), (5) and (6). Briefly, leaseholds created before 1 April 1990 must not exceed the rateable values of those subsections. Leaseholds created after that date are subject to a formula in which a notional figure reflecting the leasehold's value using the premium (not the ground rent) as a starting point must not exceed £25,000.

Since 1 November 1993, a leaseholder who fell outside the above provisions can, however, seek enfranchisement (but not an extension of the lease) under section 1A of LRA 1967.

Exclusions

There are a number of situations that are excluded from the Act which include:

1. certain shared ownership leases (the mechanisms and provisions that remove shared ownership leaseholds from the LRA 1967 are beyond the scope of this book, but see generally section 33A and Schedule 4A. See also sections 172-3 of HA 1985 which exclude shared ownership leaseholds acquired under a right to buy from the LRA 1967);
2. leasehold schemes for the elderly (as above, their exclusion from the Act is not dealt with in this book; reference should be made to a work on housing associations);
3. certain section 149(6) leases (section 1B);
4. leaseholders of charitable housing trusts (LRHUDA 1993);
5. where a Minister of the Crown certifies that the house will in ten years or less be required for relevant development (defined in section 28(6)), the leaseholder cannot serve an effective section 5 notice (see below).

Under 5. above, if a section 5 notice is served before or not later than two months after a copy of the Minister's certificate is served on the leaseholder, then the leasehold is treated as if it had been extended for section 17 purposes (see below), and the Minister's certificate is conclusive on any section 17 application (section 28).

Statutory procedures

The leaseholder starts the procedure by serving a notice under section 5 (a section 5 notice) on the landlord. The notice expresses his or her desire to enfranchise or extend the lease and contains details of the lease. The landlord has two months in which to reply and, if the decision is against the request, to state the grounds for opposition to the claim.

If the leaseholder seeks enfranchisement, the leaseholder is entitled to a conveyance of the freehold (section 8) to include the rights set out in section 10. The value is the price the property with a sitting leaseholder would fetch on the open market, without the leaseholder wishing to buy (section 9). Disputes over the freehold's valuation can be settled by the Leasehold Valuation Tribunal under section 21, with the landlord's costs to be paid by the leaseholder (section 9(4)).

Where the leaseholder wants an extended lease, the new lease must be for the unexpired term of the existing lease plus 50 years, and essentially on the same terms (section 15). Under the new lease, a ground rent must be charged which represents the site's letting value only (section 15(2)). The landlord may revise the ground rent after 25 years, for which the leaseholder is required to pay the costs.

Where the lease is extended, the new tenancy carries no further rights to enfranchise or extend. The leaseholder is no longer protected by LTA 1954 or LGHA 1989 (see above).

Landlord's opposition

A landlord has limited grounds on which to oppose a proper and valid claim and must apply to the court to establish those grounds.

A claim to enfranchise or extend can be opposed if the landlord reasonably wants the house back for his or her own or an adult family member's use (section 18). This ground is not available if

- the landlord's interest in the house was purchased or created after February 1966, or
- by upholding the opposition and passing residential possession back to the landlord, the lease-holder suffers greater hardship than if it was refused; if the landlord's opposition is upheld, the leaseholder is entitled to compensation.

A claim to extend can further be opposed if the landlord wants to demolish or reconstruct all or most of the property for redevelopment (section 17). This application can also be made by the landlord once the extension has been granted at any time not earlier than 12 months before the original lease term date.

Flats

The LRHUDA 1993 allows leaseholders to buy the freehold to their block of flats, or extended leases on their flats.

Collective enfranchisement

Qualifying leaseholders who
- have flats within that block, and
- when the section 13 notice is served (see below) on the landlord satisfy the statutory residence requirement under sections 1, 6 and 13 (see below)

can collectively acquire the freehold to their block through a nominee purchaser such as a company owned by them. The entitlement includes buying, for example, gardens and garages included in their leases (even if these are owned by a different landlord – see section 107 of HA 1996).

Qualifying leaseholders

Leaseholders must hold long, low rent leases or particularly long term leases.

A long lease is one exceeding 21 years whether terminable before the term date or not (section 7). A particularly long term is one exceeding 35 years whether terminable before the term date or not (section 8A, as inserted by Schedule 9, paragraph 3 to HA 1996). Both types of lease include perpetually renewable leases, right to buy and 100 per cent owned shared ownership leases, and section 149(6) leases.

'Low rent' is where either no rent was payable for the first year of the tenancy, or the rent did not exceed, for a lease entered into

- before 1 April 1963, two-thirds of the property's open market letting value on the date the tenancy commences;
- between 1 April 1963 and 1 April 1990, two-thirds of the property's rateable value on the first day of the term, or if later the first day the property had a rateable value; or
- on or after 1 April 1990, £1,000 in Greater London, or £250 elsewhere.

Charitable housing trust leaseholders and those holding leaseholds granted in breach of a superior leasehold's terms where the breach has not been waived do not qualify (section 5).

There can only be one qualifying leaseholder per flat at any one time. Where a leaseholder owns three or more flats within the premises (for each of which the leaseholder would be a qualifying leaseholder), the Act deems there to be no qualifying leaseholder of any of them (section 5(5)).

The premises

Under sections 3 and 4, as amended by section 107 of HA 1996, the relevant premises must

- consist of a self-contained building (or part of a building);
- contain two or more flats held by qualifying tenants; and
- the total number of flats held by such tenants is not less than two-thirds of the total number of the flats contained in the premises.

Premises are exempt if
1. the internal floor area of any part not occupied for residential purposes exceeds 10 per cent of the total internal floor area; or
2. they contain less than five units and are not purpose-built block of flats, and
   (a) the landlord or an adult family member has resided there as his or her only or principal home for 12 months, or
   (b) the landlord or his family so resided there before selling to the present landlord who moved into the house within 28 days of purchase; (an adult family member here includes a spouse, parent, parent-in-law, or child over 18 years old (section 10(5)); or
3. different, self-contained parts of the building under section 3 are owned by separate freeholders.

Procedure

A notice is served on the landlord (who is the 'reversioner' under section 9) by at least two-thirds of all qualifying lease-holders (and making up at least one-half of all flats in the block). At least half of those leaseholders must satisfy the residence condition, i.e. they must have occupied their flats for the last 12 months, or for short periods totalling three years within the last ten years (section 6(2)). The notice must include full details of:

- the nominee purchaser (whether an individual or a company), and of all leaseholders involved in it; and
- the premises and the proposed purchase price.

The nominee purchaser represents all leaseholders involved in the purchase and will acquire the premises on their behalf, and also take any proceedings arising out of the initial notice.

The landlord, under section 21, must serve a counter-notice within two months, stating that he or she:

- admits the enfranchisement is allowed;

- does not admit it and giving the reasons why, after which the nominee purchaser may apply to the court to determine the matter; or
- intends to develop the site under section 23, after which an application may be made to the court to determine the matter.

A dispute over the terms of acquisition may be settled on application to the LVT. If the sale proceeds, the landlord enters into a binding contract, or the court vests the freehold in the nominee. The leaseholders can withdraw at any time before the contract is signed (section 28). The price is the total of the value of the freeholder's interest, the freeholder's share of the marriage value (which is defined in detail in Schedule 6, paragraph 4(2) of 1993 Act), and any compensation due (section 32 and Schedule 6). The valuation formulae set out in the 1993 Act have recently been modified by HA 1996. The leaseholders must pay the landlord's costs.

Individual right to acquire new lease

Section 37 allows a qualifying leaseholder who
- owns a long, low rent leasehold flat, and
- when the section 42 notice (see below) is served on the landlord, satisfies the statutory residence requirement (section 39)

to acquire a new lease, on payment of a premium, for the unexpired term of the existing lease plus 90 years. 'Qualifying leaseholder', 'long lease' and 'low rent' have largely similar definitions as above (section 39, applying sections 5, 7 and 8). The statutory residence requirement is that he or she has lived in the flat as his or her only or principal residence for the last three years, or for short periods totalling three years over the last ten years.

Procedure

The leaseholder serves a section 42 notice on the landlord

and any other party to the lease, which must include details
of the

- leaseholder,
- flat,
- existing lease,
- proposed purchase price and terms, and
- date by which the landlord must serve a counter-notice.

The landlord's counter-notice must, under section 45, either:

- admit the leaseholder's right to extend, and state which
  of the proposed terms is accepted or rejected and put
  forward counter-proposals;
- not admit it and give reasons why, after which the
  landlord may within two months apply to the court to
  determine the matter; or
- state an intention to develop the premises under section
  47, after which the landlord may apply to the court.

Disputes over the new lease terms can be resolved on application to the LVT. The leaseholder can withdraw at any
time up to the granting of the new lease (section 52). The
price is the total value of the freeholder's interest, the freeholder's share of the marriage value, and any compensation
due (section 56 and Schedule 13). The valuation formulae set
out in the 1993 Act have recently been modified by HA 1996.
The leaseholder must pay the landlord's costs.

Right of first refusal

Leaseholders of private landlords have the right of first
refusal to buy the landlord's reversion when there is a proposed disposal of the landlord's interest in the property (Part
I of LTA 1987, as amended by HA 1996). This right is not
available at any time when the landlord's interest in the
premises is held by an exempt landlord (section 1(4)); Source
landlords are exempt landlords (section 58).

Key points

- Leaseholders occupying a house have a right under the LRA 1967 to purchase their freehold or extend their leasehold for 50 years.
- Detailed qualifying conditions must be satisfied before the right may be exercised.
- One condition (the 'low rent' condition) produces difficult and arbitrary results. The right to enfranchise may now be exercised by leaseholders with leaseholds of more than 35 years without having to satisfy this condition.
- Leaseholders with certain shared ownership leaseholds or within leasehold schemes for the elderly are excluded from the operation of the 1967 Act.
- Enfranchisement or leasehold extension is brought about through a notice procedure. There are limited grounds upon which a landlord cannot oppose a leaseholder's claim.
- Leaseholders occupying *flats* have a collective right under the LRHUDA 1993 to purchase their freehold or an individual right to extend their leasehold for 90 years.
- Detailed qualifying conditions must be satisfied before the right may be exercised.
- Collective enfranchisement is now available in situations where there are multiple freeholders within the same block.
- Collective enfranchisement or leasehold extension in a block of flats is brought about through a notice procedure. There are limited grounds upon which a landlord cannot oppose a leaseholder's claim.
- The right of first refusal under Part I of LTA 1987 is not available against social landlords.

Glossary

annual charges: charges made for regular services provided by a landlord (e.g. small items of repair and maintenance, cleaning and caretaking, maintenance of the communal parts and grounds, lighting, etc.). Compare *major works* below.

ARHM: Association of Retirement Housing Managers.

assignee: the person acquiring a property by an assignment from the previous owner (or 'assignor').

assignment: the transfer of a property right from one person to another; leaseholds and reversions may be assigned. Compare *sub-letting* below.

covenants: the terms set out in the lease that bind the landlord and leaseholder.

enfranchisement: the process by which leaseholders, individually or collectively, may be able to acquire the freehold of their house or flat.

exchange sale scheme: a scheme intended to assist leaseholders who wish to sell but there are difficulties in raising mortgage finance on the property. Under the scheme leaseholders sell their flat back to the local authority (at the discounted price that the leaseholder originally paid) and buy another flat from the local authority.

forfeiture: the process by which a landlord may terminate the leasehold if the leaseholder breaches any of his or her covenants.

freehold: a property right entitling its owner to exclusive possession of a house or flat for all time. Compare *term of years absolute*, below.

improvement: doing more work to a property than is merely required to satisfy an obligation to *repair*, see below.

initial period: a five-year period from the grant of the right to buy leasehold. It is different to the *reference period,* see below and Chapter 6.

interim charges: advance payments of service charge.

landlord (**or** *lessor* **or** *reversioner*)**:** the owner of the reversion; the person or organisation entitled to enforce covenants against the leaseholder.

lease: the document which creates the leasehold and contains all the terms agreed between the original landlord and the original lease-holder. Compare *tenancy* below.

leasehold: a term of years absolute for a substantial fixed period of time (e.g. in excess of 21 years). Compare *tenancy* below.

Leaseholders' Guarantee: guidance issued by the Housing Corporation or Housing for Wales on housing management practice for housing associations managing leaseholders.

Leasehold Valuation Tribunal: the description given to Rent Assessment Committees when performing their valuation duties under the LRA 1967. LVTs may now adjudicate disputes concerning service charges; enfranchisement of houses and flats; choice of insurer; and the appointment of a manager.

leaseholder (**or** *lessee*)**:** the owner of a leasehold.

major works: examples are cyclical redecoration and extensive works of repair or improvement. They occur infrequently and are sizeable items of expenditure. See further Chapter 5.

manager: a person appointed under Part II of LTA 1987 to assist with the management of property.

mortgage indemnity agreement: an agreement made by a local authority with a commercial lender (who has made a loan to a leaseholder and taken a mortgage to secure that loan) under which, if the leaseholder defaults on the mortgage, the local authority agree to ensure the lender is not out of pocket.

mortgagee: the person who takes a mortgage as security for a loan (i.e. the lender). Compare *mortgagor* below.

mortgagor: the owner of property who grants a mortgage over that property to another to secure a loan (i.e. the borrower).

privity of contract: the legal principle that the original landlord and original leaseholder remain bound together in contract throughout the term of the leasehold. This makes the original leaseholder liable for the performance of the covenants even after assignment of the leasehold. This legal principle has been abolished by the LT(C)A 1995 (see Chapter 10).

privity of estate: the legal principle that the covenants in the lease become 'imprinted' on both the leasehold and reversion. After assignment of the leasehold or reversion, the covenants continue to be enforceable by and against the assignee. This legal principle has been abolished by the LT(C)A 1995 although the Act substitutes a similar principle (see Chapter 10).

receiver: a person appointed under section 37 of the Supreme Court Act 1981 to assist with the management of property.

recognised tenants association: an association of leaseholders(and possibly tenants) recognised, by a notice or certificate, under section 29 of LTA 1985.

reference period: a period of 5 years, specified by the landlord, from the date (not more than six months after a section 125 notice is given) by which the landlord reasonably considers that the right to buy grant will have been made. It is different to the *initial period*, see above and Chapter 6.

repair: a technical term with precise legal meaning. In outline, the process of returning an item of property, formerly in good condition but now not so, to its former good condition. Compare *improvement* above.

reversion: the property rights vested in the landlord (e.g. a freehold or a longer leasehold than that owned by the leaseholder). The reversion gives a landlord the right to possession of the house or flat once the leasehold comes to an end.

right of alienation: the right of the owner of property (e.g. a leasehold) to transfer (or 'assign') that property right to another person. Compare *assignment* above.

right to acquire: the right of sitting tenants of some housing associations, introduced by the Housing Act 1996, to purchase the leasehold (or freehold) of their house or flat.

right to buy: a generic expression to describe the purchase by tenants of former social landlords (principally local authorities) of the leasehold (or freehold) in their house or flat. There are different types of right to buy (see Chapter 1). Compare *right to acquire* above.

Section 125 notice: the landlord's notice of purchase price and other matters served under section 125 of Housing Act 1985 on a secure tenant who is seeking to exercise his or her right to buy.

service charge: the charge made to the leaseholder for the landlord's provision of services, repairs, maintenance, insurance and/or management under the lease.

shared ownership: the purchase by a tenant of a proportion of the capital value of a flat on long leasehold. The part purchased may or may not have been funded by a mortgage. The (now) leaseholder pays a rent to the landlord in respect of the remainder of the capital value. The leaseholder may be able to purchase further shares in the equity of the flat (a process known as 'staircasing').

sinking fund: the collection of advance payments made for the payment of service charge in a future year when there will be major works (and therefore a dramatic hike in the service charge payable that year).

sub-letting: where the owner of a leasehold (or tenancy) grants a smaller leasehold (or tenancy) to another. By contrast, *assignment* (see above) is where the owner transfers the whole of his or her property right to another.

superior landlord: the landlord's landlord (e.g. a freeholder or a leaseholder with a longer leasehold than that owned by the landlord). The superior landlord is entitled to possession of the house or flat once the landlord's leasehold comes to an end.

tenancy: a term of years absolute that is a short term letting arrangement, usually periodic in nature (e.g. a weekly tenancy or secure and assured tenancies). Sometimes statutes confusingly use the word 'tenancy' or 'lease' to describe a leasehold. In this book, unless pointed out to the reader, these words have the meaning set out in this glossary. Compare *lease* and *leasehold* above.

tenant: a person who has a tenancy.

term of years absolute: a property right entitling its owner to exclusive possession of a house or flat for a defined period of time (see LPA 1925, section 1(1)(b)). Leaseholds and tenancies are both within this definition.

Index

OTHER BOOKS AVAILABLE IN ARDEN'S HOUSING LIBRARY

Security of Tenure

Law and practice in the management of social housing
Andrew Dymond, Barrister

"readable . . . up-to-date, it includes well chosen examples and a helpful appendix." *The Adviser*

All housing managers know their way around the law on security of tenure. Or do they? What are the conditions that have to be met to make a tenancy secure? Exactly what steps should be taken before starting proceedings against tenants who are in arrears with rent? For experienced practitioners, this book is that indispensable companion which will always provide guidance in moments of doubt. For those approaching the subject for the first time, it is an invaluable summary of the law.

Contents include:

Status of the Occupier • Tenant or Licensee? • Secure and Assured Tenancies • Conditions for Security of Tenure • Seeking Possession • Grounds for Possession Against Secure Tenants • Grounds for Possession Against Assured Tenants • Suitable Alternative Accommodation • Reasonableness • Other Occupiers • Possession Orders • Termination by the Tenant

Arden's Housing Library vol.1
Paperback   172pp   216 x 138mm   ISBN 1-898001-12-X

Tenants' Rights

Law and practice in the management of social housing
Caroline Hunter, Nottingham University

**"Caroline Hunter has written very clearly and concisely and made
extremely good use of case law, which is presented in
a way that brings the text alive."** *The Adviser*

Tenants' rights are a new area of law. Beginning in 1980, these rights have
been swiftly developed and expanded. Secure tenants of councils and housing
associations now have more control over their homes than ever before. So
keeping abreast of tenants' rights is now essential for anyone working in the
housing field – and this book is the way to do it.

As individuals, many tenants may now take in lodgers, exchange their
homes or even sublet them. Often other family members can succeed to a
tenancy. Collectively family members have new rights to information, to
manage their own homes and even to change their landlord.

Contents include:

Historical background • Succession • Assignment, Lodgers and Subletting
• Changing the Terms of the Tenancy • Information and Consultation
• The Right to Manage • Estate Redevelopment

Arden's Housing Library vol.2
Paperback   136pp   216 x 138mm   ISBN 1-898001-13-8

Presenting Possession Proceedings
Law and practice in the management of social housing
Andrew Dymond, Barrister

"Housing managers and officers involved in regaining possession should find this book invaluable." *ADC Review*

It can be unpleasant. It is certainly not easy but it has to be done. Sooner or later every social landlord is faced with taking back possession of a tenant's home when rent arrears have run out of control, when nuisance has become intolerable or when the tenant has disappeared leaving friends or relatives in residence.

With pressure to maximise rent income and minimise management costs, more and more housing managers and officers are going to find themselves handling the ensuing possession proceedings. Checklists are included to make sure proceedings will not run into the sand because of error or omission.

Contents include:
Commencing Possession Proceedings • What Needs to be Proved?
• The Return Date • Pre-Trial Procedure • Evidence • The Trial • Rent Arrears Cases • Other Types of Possession Action • Possession Orders
• Further Action • Court Forms

Arden's Housing Library vol.4
Paperback   200pp   216 x 138mm   ISBN 1-898001-15-4

Repairs and Maintenance
Law and practice in the management of social housing
Alyson Kilpatrick, Barrister

"...an admirably concise but thorough exposition of the principles of the law in this area. The author, while impartial, is realistic about the problems faced by social landlords and practical in her advice..." *Housing Agenda*

Disrepair in Britain's ageing social housing stock is already a problem – and it's getting worse. Shortage of money often leaves landlords unable to attend to repairs. But not doing repairs can be even more costly – as buildings deteriorate further and tenants, denied the comfort and security of their homes, go to court.

This book provides landlords with a practical understanding of their own legal obligations and those of their tenants. Covering problem areas like condensation, this guide follows the process through, looking at the landlord's powers to get work done, and the role of housing staff when all else fails and court proceedings begin.

Contents include:
Social Landlord's Contractual Liabilities • Common Types of Complaint
• Tenants' Remedies • Public Health Duties • Tenants' Contractual Obligations
• Getting the Works Done • Improvements • Court Proceedings
• Compendium of Damages Awards • Sample Legal Pleadings
• Best Practice Checklists

Arden's Housing Library vol.5
Paperback   240pp   216 x 138mm   ISBN 1-898001-11-1

Dealing with Disrepair
A guide to inspection and diagnosis
Patrick Reddin, FRICS, FBEng

"The technical information is simply and clearly presented with useful building diagrams...its methodical approach will make it particularly useful as a training tool for both landlord and tenant." *Housing Agenda*

"...a valuable contribution to raising standards and customer care, efficiency and effectiveness..."
Royal Institution of Chartered Surveyors' president

Understanding buildings is something which is usually left up to surveyors. It shouldn't be. Millions of people suffer as a result of serious disrepair in their home. To remedy this quickly, housing managers need to understand the buildings their tenants are living in, accurately define what repair is needed and know how to get work done. This guide breaks new ground. It includes over 30 detailed cross-section drawings and good practice checklists.

Arden's Housing Library vol.6
Paperback   232 pp   216 x 138mm   illustrated
ISBN 1-898001-06-5

Compulsory Competitive Tendering of Housing Management

Law and practice in the management of social housing

Caroline Hunter and Andy Selman

Clearly setting out the legal framework, this book goes through each step in contracting the service from first drafts, through advertising and letting, to monitoring and re-specifying. The organisation of in-house bids get special attention, while the background and possible future direction of CCT are not forgotten.

Here to help local authorities through the process, this guide offers invaluable support to staff letting and monitoring the contracts. But it also provides essential information for the tenants whose views must be taken into account, the workforce whose jobs are at stake, and the councillors who are ultimately responsible for the contracts let. For any housing department trying to make CCT work to the best advantage, this is the book.

Arden's Housing Library vol.7

Paperback   176 pp   216 x 138mm   ISBN 1-898001-05-7

Rights to Buy and Acquire

Law and practice in the management of social housing
Josephine Henderson, Barrister

"This book will be essential reading and reference for any housing professional with the thankless task of administering sales to tenants... the step-by-step guide to procedures in Chapter 4 is worth the purchase price by itself." *Agenda*

Council and some housing assocation tenants have had the Right to Buy their homes for nearly 20 years. A new Right to Acquire has been introduced for the tenants of housing associations and other registered social landlords. Meanwhile as problems surface from the early burst of sales activity in the 1980s an accessible guide to the legal process that underpins these rights has been lacking. This book fills the gap.

Contents include:
Who has the Right to Buy? • Qualifications and Exceptions • What is Bought?
• Procedure • The Price and Paying It • The Grant or Conveyance
• Loss and Enforcement of Right to Buy • Changes in the Landlord's Interest
• Extension of Right • Housing Associations and Other Registered Social Landlords

Arden's Housing Library vol.8
Paperback   192pp   216 x 138mm   ISBN 1-898001-15-4

Lemos & Crane books are obtainable from good bookshops or directly from

Plymbridge Distributors Ltd

Estover Road, Plymouth PL6 7PZ

• Tel: 01752 202301

• Fax: 01752 202333

Information about Arden's Housing Library and other Lemos & Crane books is available from

Lemos & Crane

20 Pond Square, London N6 6BA

• Tel: 0181-348 8263

• Fax: 0181-347 5740